Sul

Rome

i piccoli
di arsenale

Ivana Della Portella

Subterranean Rome

Photographs
Mark E. Smith

arsenale e⧸t editrice

Ivana Della Portella
SUBTERRANEAN ROME

Photographs
Mark E. Smith

Translation from the Italian
Richard Pierce

Printed and bound by
EBS Editoriale Bortolazzi-Stei
Verona

Second edition
November 2012

Arsenale Editore Srl
Via Monte Comun, 40
I - 37057 San Giovanni Lupatoto (VR)

© *2012 Arsenale Editrice*

ISBN 978-88-7743-281-0

Photograph credits

Archivio Fotografico «Forma Urbis»,
Roma, pp. 30, 42, 60, 65, 68, 98, 104,
108, 117, 122, 142, 152, 158, 159,
170, 174, 178, 186
Archivio Fotografico Museo di Palazzo
Massimo, Roma, pp. 113, 163
Archivio Fotografico Scala, Firenze,
pp. 107, 165, 177, 179
Archivio Fotografico suore Benedettine,
Roma, pp. 68-71, 145-148
Biblioteca Nazionale Marciana, Venezia
pp. 8, 49, 56, 75, 92
Humberto N. Serra, Roma, pp. 8, 11
Istituto Nazionale per la Grafica, Roma,
(n. i. F. N. 6695) p. 109
Pino Agostini, Verona, p. 73

*The publisher would like to thank the
following for their kind assistance:*
Padri Domenicani Irlandesi (complesso
di San Clemente, pp. 37-39, 126-131)
Padri Carmelitani (San Martino ai
Monti, pp. 132-135)
Padri Passionisti (Santi Giovanni e
Paolo, pp. 136-139)

Table of Contents

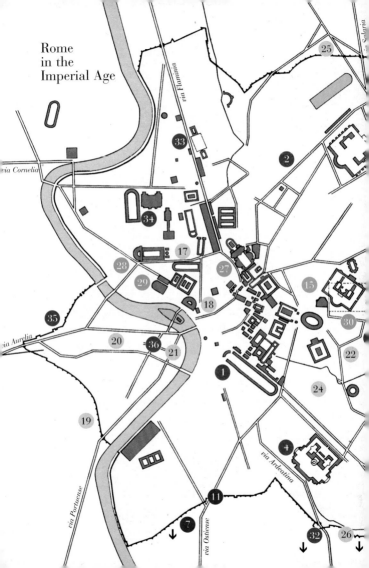

Rome
in the
Imperial Age

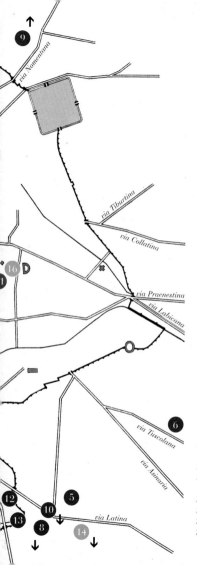

KEY

Top: a fragment of the Forma Urbis.
Above: fragments of the Forma Urbis *(engraving by Piranesi).*

Introduction

There is a bewitching Rome above the ground that captivates visitors with its fascinating colours and views. Its sky is by no means ordinary, and the urban scenery makes this city a veritable theatre, with its spectacular domes, obelisks and fountains as backdrops.

Then, under the splendid vestiges of various ages and styles, is a "subterranean" Rome made up of everyday life and things that are perhaps less appealing than the "archaeology above ground". Consequently, this "other" Rome is virtually unknown to most people. And yet it offers a rare spectacle of lights and colours that create a truly unique "lower" world.

It is a labyrinth of the past with traces of a civilization that has left us colossal architectural works that still tower over the city–arches, temples, columns. But that same civilization has also bequeathed us a "minor" Rome under the ground that may be less theatrical and grandiose but is certainly no less fascinating and evocative, where all the richness and *vulgaritas* of daily life can be read in the stones. This is an area yet to be explored, and in some cases you will discover remains whose artistic and architectural quality is equal to that of the monuments above the ground. This will be a journey into darkness, or, as Tertullian said about the Mithraic sanctuaries, into the domains of darkness (*castra tenetrarum*), to find the roots of a buried, or partly excavated, civilization that for the most part did not originate under the ground but was buried by the deposits of centuries of history. Mithraea, columbaria, storehouses, barracks and hypogea tell the story of this subterranean world and mark out the stages of our journey far from the erudite Latin of the forums. Here we will find a more corrupted, colloquial language that reveals the needs and beliefs of "banal," everyday life, the superstitions and rites that are out of the ordinary, hidden, deliberately relegated under the ground. We will see lavish *domus* and modest *insulae*, service rooms and sanctuaries: a multifarious panorama that offers a virtually infinite gamut of settings and contexts.

In the mithraeum of the Circus Maximus we can discover the sacred image of one of the most ancient Middle Eastern cults, and it will not be difficult to visualize the faithful taking part in the rituals, walking to the rhythm of the *tintinnabulum* (little bell) or testing their endurance and courage in the initiation ceremonies.

While walking among the broad arcades of the Stadium of Domitian, we can rediscover the world of ancient sports and recreate its exciting atmosphere. In the columbarium of Pomponius Hylas there is an evocation of the ancient vision of the afterlife and of the Orphic mysteries, whose graceful and gay representation of the underworld turns the darkness of death into a playful setting of stuccowork and dazzling colours.

In Via Livenza we can experience the rather disturbing mixture of a burgeoning Christianity and paganism in its death throes. It is not easy to know whether the small basin at the end of the hall was used for the meek ablutions of the early Christians or for immersion by the dissolute *Baptai*, devotees of an orgiastic mystery cult.

The subterrean areas of S. Paolo alla Regola, on the other hand, have the colours and smells of a lively commercial neighbourhood, with the daily life of common people and their humble and decrepit apartment blocks. And at Trastevere we will find traces of the activities of the militia or civic guards, their barracks (*excubitorium*), as well as the graffiti they wrote on the walls, like ancient voices and images of their daily life: tallow torches, *siphones* water pumps, the lack of water, and the fear of that terrible enemy, fire.

This journey can by no means include all the vast and variegated panorama of subterranean Rome, but aims rather at providing a cross-section that best embodies it. The approach is based on erudition and research but is not too "academic" or technical, so that the quality of the information will not detract in any way from what could be described as a subliminal relationship between readers and text; that is to say, the voices of the obscure past, which have so much to say about those stones buried under centuries of history, can be evoked and heard again.

A model of Rome during the Imperial Age.

Mithraism

Christianity was a new religion when the cult of Mithra, with its strong accent on mysteries, revived a paganism that was clearly in decline. From the outset, these two monotheistic religions manifested many points in common and both performed rituals and liturgies based on redemption and catharsis. However, while the former had an ecumenical approach and addressed everyone, the latter was reserved for an élite of initiates. This difference is by no means insignificant, since through the centuries it determined the demise of the more exclusive, mystical and esoteric religion, Mithraism.

The Spread of the Cult

Mithraism, which originated in Persia, was named after the Indo-Iranian god Mithra (known as Mithras in ancient Rome), who in his first Eastern configuration appears as a solar god, the guarantor of pacts among tribes, the god of oaths, contracts and all those conventions of social life that ensure peace and stability in agricultural settlements.

Already in ancient Persia these solar and propitiatory attributes were gradually transformed and the god took on a bellicose, military character, which is the one that prevailed in the West when Mithraism spread through the Roman Empire.

When the cult of Mithra was "exported" to Greece thanks to some

Opposite: marble relief of the bull sacrifice in the Circus Maximus mithraeum.

pirates from Cilicia whom Pompey had deported in 67 B.C., it was an immediate success because of its initiatory and redemptive nature, soon spreading to the entire Mediterranean region and into northern Europe.

When it made its appearance in the West, the cult differed greatly from its original Eastern form. Through a complicated process of development, the original Persian and Indo-Aryan elements of Zoroastrianism (or Mazdaism) were replaced by later Chaldaean-Babylonian doctrines and the magical-religious disciplines of the Zoroastrian priests. The Roman cult of Mithra was therefore the result of a syncretic process whereby the god acquired a character quite different from his original one, in which the mystical, mysterious and redemptive aspects prevailed. It was at its height in the 3rd century A.D. and then lost ground to the rising Christian religion at the end of the 4th century, during the decline of the Western Roman Empire.

The Myth of Mithra

To gain a better idea of the message that lay behind the sacred images of the Mithraic caves and understand the many painted or stucco representations in the Persian god's sanctuaries, his myth should be known.

One day Mithra, a young and handsome god, emerged from the solid vault of the heavens in the form of light. *Invictus de petra natus*: the generating stone had given birth to him on the banks of a river, in the shade of a sacred tree. Some shepherds in the vicinity witnessed this miraculous birth. They saw the god come out of the rock naked, armed with a knife and with a torch in his hand and a Phrygian bonnet on his head. They offered him shelter and gifts and worshipped him. From the time of his birth, Mithra began his heroic deeds, whose purpose was to defeat "cosmic" evil. First he faced the Sun (Sol) who, defeated, made a pact with Mithra and gave him his radiant crown (which became one of his attributes). Then there was the episode of the wild bull. Mithra captured the bull and took it to his cave (*specus*), after which he had to face a series of obstacles in his path (*transitus*). However, the bull managed to escape and was seen by the Sun, who sent his messenger the Raven to give Mithra the order to slay the bull, an ungrateful task that the god performed reluctantly. First he followed the bull's tracks, aided by his faithful dog, and as the bull was about to take shelter in the cave it had escaped from, he seized it by the nostrils and thrust a knife into its side (*tauroctonia*). Only then did the body of the dying bull miraculously give birth to all the plants beneficial to Man, which spread throughout the Earth: wheat emerged from its spine and grapevines from its blood. Ahriman, the god of evil, who could not remain passive before this plenitude of life, sent his wicked helpers, the scorpion and serpent, to check the flow of these vital elements. In vain: neither the scorpion nor the serpent managed to stop the bull's seed from spreading. Thus, after its purification it could ascend to the Moon, giving rise to all the useful species of animals. Mithra and the Sun sealed this victory with a feast (*agape*) and then went on the Sun's

Triclinium in the Circus Maximus mithraeum used for the agape *(sacred banquet).*

chariot toward the sky, whence Mithra continued to protect his faithful worshippers.

The Mithraic Caves

The cult of Mithra was performed inside grottoes and natural or artificial caves (*specus*). Apart from any fascination for the horrible and tenebrous, the choice of dark places reflected a precise symbolic configuration that the following passage by the ancient Greek scholar Porphyry may clarify: "Zarathustra was the first one who dedicated to Mithra, the father of all things, a natural cave situated in the nearby Persian mountains [...], for him the cave embodied the image of the cosmos, of which Mithra is the demiurge, and the objects placed in it at calculated intervals were symbols of the cosmic elements and the regions of the sky."

The Mithraic cave was therefore selected for astrological reasons, inasmuch as it was an allegory of the cosmos: "Rightly," Porphyry writes, "the ancients dedicated caves and caverns to the cosmos [...] since for them the earth was the symbol of the matter of which the cosmos is made [...], and, what is more, they believed the caves represented the cosmos that has taken shape from matter." Consequently, one must reject the scornful accusation of Tertullian, who called the Mithraea "domains of darkness" (*castra tenebrarum*), as opposed to the Christians' *castra lucis* (domains of light), for he considered them places where diabolical and blasphemous rites were practised, in a sort of malignant imitation of the Christian ritual. "And they call this Mithra, and celebrate his liturgy in hidden grottoes, where, deep in the obscure and wretched darkness, they can escape the benediction of the shining sun [...] oh detestable invention of a barbarous practice!" Such invective shows that the Christian apologists did not understand the underlying reasons for this choice, which emphasized the contradiction between the solar nature of the god and his dark, subterranean sanctuary. Mithra *invictus de petra natus*, in fact, was born on the day of the *natalis solis* (December 25). He had made an alliance with the Sun and had acquired his radiant crown and principal life-giving virtues, thus becoming a sun god in all respects. Why then did he choose dark and oppressive caves as his place of worship?

The question only seems to be contradictory. As Porphyry pointed out, the Mithraic caves had a precise symbolic meaning, being a clear-cut allusion to the cosmos and the movement of the planets. This symbolism, which seems to have escaped the notice of its Christian adversaries, was in fact part and parcel of Mithraic thought, which was deeply rooted in Chaldaean-Babylonian astrological concepts. Indeed, Mithraism was a syncretic religion that could be practised on different levels. From the lowest stage of worship, the faithful could proceed gradually toward a more complex form of astrological exegesis that was reserved for a limited number of devotees at the highest stages of initiation.

The Astrological Meanings

The passage from Porphyry also tells us that in Mithraism the cosmos was divided into symbolic meanings of an astrological nature. This division alluded to a passage in stages, the same one the soul

S. Clemente mithraeum: the worshippers' meeting room.

was to make on its otherworldly journey. Celsus maintained that the Mithraic mysteries taught the symbolic correlations between the two celestial revolutions–that of the fixed stars and that of the planets– and the "circular journey of the soul through them."

The idea of the journey of the soul through the cosmos was common to many religions based on Neo-Platonism. "I arrived at the frontier of death," writes Apuleius, "and set foot on the threshold of Proserpine's kingdom; during my return I was transported through all the elements of the cosmos." However, in Mithraism this idea took on an especially important role by orienting the choices of the believer (*miste*) toward an interior journey to salvation, a passage that was to be made in stages by means of a progressive, seven-level initiation. The first one was the Raven (*Corax*); the second, the Occult (*Cryphius* or *Nymphius*, Nymph); the third, the Soldier (*Miles*); the fourth, the Lion (*Leo*); the fifth, the Persian (*Perses*); the sixth, the Sun messenger (*Heliodromus*); and the seventh and last, the Father (*Pater*). This individual catharsis was the exemplification of the same quest on the part of the soul.

These seven stages were associated with the seven gates, the seven planetary spheres, the seven days of the week and the seven metals. The Moon (silver) was assigned to the first gate, Mercury (iron) to the second, Venus (tin) to the third, Sun (gold) to the fourth, Mars (alloy) to the fifth, Jupiter (bronze) to the sixth and Saturn (lead) to the seventh. The signs of the Zodiac were in turn associated with the planets, in a complex and osmotic series of sacred interrelationships. In making its journey to the supreme sky, the soul had to pass through seven celestial spheres (the seven planets), thus freeing itself from the astral influence of the planets crossed, the same influences the soul had received when it had to make the passage in the opposite direction, on its descent to the Earth. The soul would have to rid itself of its vital and nutritional energy when passing through the Moon, its greed when passing through Mercury, its erotic impulses on Venus, its intellect on the Sun, its war-like ardour on Mars, its ambition on Jupiter and, lastly, its sloth when passing through

Opposite: the triclinium in the S. Clemente Mithraic temple.

Saturn. This journey of purification, in which the soul stripped itself of its passions, was symbolized by the devotee in the various progressive stages of his initiation.

The trials of endurance the initiates had to go through to gain access to the superior levels are unknown to us, except for vague references according to which the neophyte had to jump blindfolded over a pit and with his hands tied with chicken entrails, or witness simulated murders. At any rate, the aim of these trials was to demonstrate the devotees' mastery of sentiment and emotions that would lead to a form of self-control much like the Stoics' apathy.

During the ceremony the initiates wore animal masks that corresponded to their stage of initiation. For example, if they were in the Lion stage they would behave like a lion. The rationale for the masked devotees' behaviour was a form of identification of the animal with the god. For that matter, the pivotal act of the cult of Mithra was animal sacrifice, albeit elevated to a level of cosmic and universal salvation.

The Rituals

The candidates' admission ceremony had an extremely solemn hieratic character: "When one of these is initiated in a grotto [...]", writes Tertullian, "a crown is proffered to him on the tip of a sword: the ritual is a sort of counterfeit martyrdom. And after the crown has been securely placed on his head, he is invited to take it off with a gesture of refusal and to move it, as the case may be, to his shoulder, declaring that Mithra alone is his crown. From that day on he no longer wears crowns on his head; and symbolically this is like an attribute of his, so that should by chance his oath of loyalty to the army be challenged, he will immediately be considered a soldier of Mithra, since he has cast off the crown and said that it lies within his god."

In the darkness of the Mithraic caves barely illuminated by twinkling torches and candles, the initiates celebrated their ritual in honour of the god Mithra. They sang solemn songs and hymns to him in a shamanic-like state of intoxication, exultation and transport that was partly induced by drinking *haoma*. "Oh golden

Haoma, I ask of thee wisdom, strength and victory, health and recovery, prosperity and greatness, bodily strength and knowledge of all things; and may I pass through the world as the absolute master, crushing all evil." The devotees had to perform purification ablutions much like Christian baptism, the procedure of which is unknown to us but must have been connected to the various initiation stages. Furthermore, there was a banquet, the Mithraic *agape*, which was eaten with bread and wine.

The obvious analogy with the Eucharist alarmed the Christians, who warned against the dangers of a demonic falsification. "To imitate us," Justin wrote, "the wicked demons have ordered their devotees to do the same [as the Eucharist] in the mysteries

Barberini mithraeum: detail of the fresco with the myth of Mithras.

of Mithra, for bread and a goblet of water are presented in the initiation ceremonies with certain formulas that you know or can learn." Unfortunately, these formulas are not known, although some scholars claim they have discovered them in a papyrus kept in the Bibliothèque Nationale in Paris.

The choice of a banquet as a pivotal ritual act in the Mithraic liturgy sanctioned the final act of sacrifice of the bull through the partaking of the bread, produced by the blood and spinal marrow of the bull. In the myth, when the young god with a Phrygian bonnet thrusts his blade into the crop of the ferocious and powerful animal, a grapevine issues from its blood and ears of wheat spring miraculously from its tail. This is a form of theological sublimation of some archaic agrarian sacrifice in which a bull was sacrificed every year to guarantee the growth of plants, especially wheat. This vision of fertility was accompanied by another of an eschatological nature that was linked with the beginning and end of the world.

The Tauroctonia

A relief or painting of a sacred image occupied a central place in Mithraic caves: an image fraught with meaning that was meant to embody the entire religious and symbolic paradigm of Mithraism. The figure depicted is a young god with golden hair barely kept in place by a Phrygian cap and with a broad flapping cloak who sinks a long knife into the crop of a brawny and recalcitrant bull. A dog and a serpent are licking the bull's blood and a scorpion, moving toward the animal's testicles, tries to gather its fecund seed. This is the culminating moment of the myth: the *tauroctonia* or taurocide, the sacrifice of the bull.

For the initiates to the Mithraic mysteries, the victory over the wild bull signified the dominion of order over primeval barbarism as well as its inevitable evolution towards human civilization. Not everyone was able to grasp the intimate nature, subtleties and implications of cosmological and astrological thought. Only an exclusive circle, which belonged to the upper grades of initiation, could comprehend the

Opposite: the Sun with the radiant crown of the bull sacrifice.

more complex concepts that endowed Mithra with demiurgic powers. By killing the primordial bull, Mithra created the universe. That act triggered the movement of the planets, which with their celestial rotation gave life to Time.

Inexorable Time

The notion of Time as an unlimited entity (Zurvan Akarana) was already a part of Mazdean throught and took on a primary role in Mithraism. Astrological belief maintained that the movement of the planets and signs of the Zodiac inexorably conditioned the course of the universe. Time, which expressed itself through the deterministic action of the planetary influences, therefore acquired its attribute of inevitability, constituting the tragic aspect of Mithraic thought, as was the case with other contemporary fatalistic schools of thought of the same period, such as Stoicism.

In many Mithraea archaeologists have found the statue of a lion-headed monster (Zurvan, Kronos, Saturn) which symbolizes the qualities of Time, its omnivorous nature and all-too-rapid passage. It is an awesome image, at once human and bestial, with wings, a lion's head, and its body wrapped in a serpent's coils. The wings stand for the speed of Time, the lion's head with its gaping jaws, Time's voracity. The coils of the serpent symbolize the cyclical movement of the stars and heavens that govern the flow of time. "The movement of the sun, although never deviating from an elliptical course, yet pushes upwards or downwards with variations determined by the changing direction of the winds, following a path that is similar to a serpent's coils," says Macrobius. On the serpent, or elsewhere, the monster bears the signs of the Zodiac, and at times the signs of the seasons as well. It is also holding a sceptre and thunderbolt in its capacity as a sovereign god. It often holds one or two keys, too, a reference to the sun, which during its daily journey opens and closes the gates of the sky, to the East when it rises and to the West when it sets. Therefore, it is Time that makes and destroys all things, the lord and master of the four elements of the cosmos, that which contains the power of all the gods which it alone has generated.

Three-fold Mithra

Together with the horrible figure of the lion-headed Kronos in the sanctuary, there were statues or bas-reliefs of two young men who resembled the young Persian god to a "T", with his cloak and Phrygian cap. The two, known as *Cautes* and *Cautopates*, or as the torchbearers, are often found on either side of Mithra in the bull immolation scene. One of them raises his torch, while the other's is lowered, and with Mithra they form a triad, the three-fold Mithra. These are manifestations of the god that were arranged so as to allude to the solar cycle: dawn (Cautes, with the raised torch), noon (Mithra) and sunset (Cautopates, with the lowered torch). They also represent the two extremities of being, the heat of life and the bitter cold of death.

After this introduction we can now view the Mithraic caves with an adequate knowledge of the Mithraic religion and interpret the many

Circus Maximus mithraeum: the serpent and dog in the tauroctonia *scene.*

signs and images that decorate its ancient sanctuaries. Going into these underground recesses is like making a journey backwards in time, an unforgettable experience in some respects. This is especially true if we have a store of historical and other information that will help us to imagine those rough, bare walls eroded by time reverberating with an arcane, mysterious cult whose initiation rites are quite similar to the liturgies of present-day esoteric sects.

Not many mithraea have survived in the West, but Rome has a large number of them. Of these, only a few are open to the public, often only with special permission. Despite this, they are a fascinating testimony of the past, made even more intriguing by their harsh underground ambiance. We must remember that the Mithraic sanctuaries were founded below ground level, often at several metres' depth, for religious reasons. In the best of cases, access is afforded by steps, many of which are ancient.

As we have seen, the choice of a dark underground site was in keeping with a precise symbology related to an exclusive, élitist approach to religion. Almost all of them are artificial chambers that were made to resemble caves through special expedients, such as the use of pumice stone. They are usually rectangular (or at least the main chamber is), with long benches on the sides where the faithful sat to partake of the Mithraic *agape* banquet. These chambers are surrounded by others with specific functions such as a vestibule, *schola* and *apparitorium* (in most cases they were used for other purposes in a later period).

So let us imagine the initiates entering these dark caves faintly lit by a few torches. The rays of light illuminate the most important sacred images to create a proper solemn setting for the worshippers, focusing on the central image of the tauroctonia, the disturbing representation of the lion-headed monster, and the statues of the torchbearers. We can hear their songs and hymns and, perhaps, catch a glimpse of someone wearing the Raven's mask, whirling about madly and cawing loudly under the intoxicating effect of the *haoma* drink. We can also see the Pater ringing the little bell (*tintinnabulum*) as he unveils the sacred image of the bull-slaying god, and then observe him while he keeps watch over the sacred flame.

Now these damp caves are filled with the echoes of a long-lost liturgy: amid a strong smell of *haoma* and incense a host of masked men has wine and bread; then the light is extinguished and that smell is covered by the bitter odor of blood. A bull has been sacrificed to a Persian god in the name of cosmic and individual salvation. Its life-giving blood drips from the grating and pours down over the adept: this is the *taurobolium*, the baptismal bath, of his initiation.

The songs cease and the frenetic agitation that dominated a few moments earlier gives way to absolute silence, the perfect atmosphere for the group of men to meditate on their destiny, in their quest for a moment of immortality.

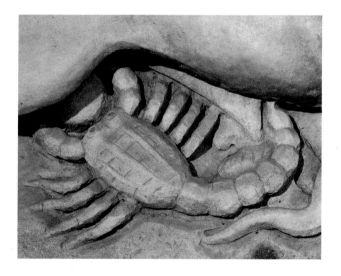

The Circus Maximus mithraeum: the scorpion in the tauroctonia *scene.*

1 – The Circus Maximus Mithraeum

Not far from the Bocca della Verità, beneath the former Pantanella pastry shop (now the Rome Opera's costume storeroom), there is an enchanting atmosphere of ancient initiation rituals. Several metres below street level, in fact, is a mithraeum, a hypogean sanctuary connected to the cult of Mithra that was built in a vast 2nd-century A.D. public building facing the *carceres* of the Circus Maximus. In the 3rd century B.C. this was the meeting place of a small group of followers of the ancient Indo-Iranian religion who set up their sanctuary in an underground chamber. Access to this Mithraic *spelaeum* is by a long narrow stairway. The first thing one sees, at right, is a small room with a niche dressed in marble. Given its position and shape, it can reasonably be considered an *apparitorum*, a sort of sacristy. At the end of the atrium, in a prominent position, are two recesses situated opposite one another that are now empty. What did these niches house? Their location at the entrance leaves no room for doubt: they were certainly for the statues of the two inseparable companions of the invincible Mithra, Cautes and Cautopates, that is to say, the three-fold Mithra.

In the next chamber there are the usual *podia*, the benches where the worshippers sat during the ceremonies celebrating the sacred banquet, the Mithraic *agape*. The bench has a shelf that was useful for placing the food, wine and oil-lamps.

In the following room are two more niches. In the right-hand one is a built-in terracotta vessel that may have been used for the lustral water necessary for baptism. The niches are dressed in painted plaster and were originally decorated with aedicules, which lent a monumental atmosphere to the underground house of worship.

Below the grandiose arch that affords access to the main part of the sanctuary –the Mithraic *sancta sanctorum*–an alabaster circle breaks the monotony of a pavement made of reused marble taken from older constructions, a flash of bright colour among the veins of cipolin, dull grey marble and coralline breccia. Further on is a circular open-

Opposite: overall view of the Mithraic cave.

cular opening that once housed an amphora in which some pig bones
and two teeth were found. Evidently this cavity, which originally had
a marble cover, was in some way connected to the liturgy.

Opposite this is a remarkably large marble relief depicting the tau-
rocton. The Moon and Sun seem to be witnessing the scene, and
Mithra, whose mantle is being held by the Raven's beak, is looking at
the Sun. The god's act is framed by Cautes and Cautopates, on either
side. What seems to characterize the relief is the appearance, at left,
of the so-called *transitus*, the moment when Mithra, having captured
the bull, takes it into the cave. Why did the donor of the relief want
to emphasize this scene? The inscription above the relief tells us it was
Tiberius Claudius Hermes, who also may have chosen the subject.
The *transitus* had a precise symbolic meaning–the celebration of the
initiation trials. So it may very well be that Tiberius Claudius Hermes
also wanted his gift to convey the great difficulty of the initiation.

A large arch, whose intrados is dressed in pumice stone, divides the
main area of the Mithraic triclinium and marks off the section with
the most idols. A series of differently shaped bases, whose function is

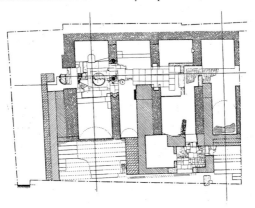

Plan of the Mithraic sanctuary.

is unknown, surrounds this sacred treasury, suggesting how rich its furnishings and decoration (which no longer exist) must have been. While it is most likely that the two bases at the sides of the arch were used to house the statues of the Sun and Moon, the functions of the other bases are more difficult to ascertain. Inside, an aedicule, which in ancient times was dressed in brilliant marble, must have been the sacred receptacle of the god's statuette. At left above the arch, next to two large corbels that must have supported a lintel, are barely legible ancient graffiti: an unclear message that has not yet been fully interpreted, but which reveals in no uncertain terms the importance attached to the magic arts. The word *magicas* carved on the wall tells us there was a close relationship between that small group of devotees and the Persian Magi, or better, with the Magusai. These Zoroastrian priests, with the contribution of astrology, theosophy and the Chaldaean-Babylonian magical-syncretic disciplines, adopted and transformed the Zoroastrian Mithra into the character of the Roman Mithras. On the right-hand side of the arch is another small relief with the usual representation of the bull sacrifice.

Marble relief depicting the immolation of the bull (tauroctonia).

2 – The Barberini Mithraeum

Hidden among the delightful paths in the Barberini Garden is a mithraeum. Just past the palazzo, a broad ramp goes up to the Savorgnan di Brazzà villa (1936), which contains the ancient *spelaeum*. A stairway leads to this cave, which is really a small underground building constructed in different periods. It is rectangular, with a barrel vault and lateral podia, and occupies one of the three rooms found while the villa was being built. The low vault presses down on the hall, accentuating its gloomy character. On one of the piers is a female figure whose pose can be interpreted as an offering. The benches for worshippers slope downward toward the walls and have the usual ledges. An inscription on the right-hand bench gives us the name of the donor: "Iperante has offered the base to the indomitable god Mithra."

In the middle, an altar that is perforated to allow smoke to escape evokes the figure of the Pater–the highest degree of initiation and priesthood–who was charged with tending to the eternal flame. He also prayed to the Sun three times a day, facing the cardinal points, sacrificed the animals and collected their blood in a pit, and presided over the libations and the cult rituals.

But it is the fresco on the back wall that dominates the cave. The figure of the god slaying the bull, accompanied by the symbolic torchbearers, stands out against a light background. A glance at the upper register reveals some interesting elements that characterize this representation: a large, semicircular band bears the signs of the Zodiac with the figure of Kronos in the middle. The lion-headed monster appears as the lord of the universe and the influence of the planets, wrapped in the coils of the serpent, while he is towering over the sphere of the universe. Above, the Sun and Moon observe this sequence of signs, as though they were watching the movement of the cosmos created by Mithra. The god's cloak is decorated with seven stars representing the fixed stars. By killing the cosmic bull Mithra created the universe and the movement of his cloak gave rise to the rotation of the fixed stars.

Opposite: Mithras killing the bull.

The planets began to move in the opposite direction, following the path marked out by the constellations of the Zodiac. Therefore Time, whose rhythm is marked by the rotation of the stars, was born from the sacrifice effected by Mithra.

The central scene is flanked by ten smaller ones divided into two lateral bands that relate Mithra's mythical feats. On the left-hand side, the first scene illustrates Jupiter brandishing a lightning bolt to strike an anguiped giant, which refers to the battle between Zeus and the Titans. The second scene represents a recumbent female figure that can be interpreted as the *Terra Mater* fecundated by the waters of *Coelus* to give life to *Oceanus*. In the third scene, Mithra is being born from a rock, holding a knife and a torch and accompanied by the torchbearers. The fourth scene shows Mithra shooting an arrow to strike the rock, with an adept nearby waiting to quench his thirst. This episode, which is analogous to the one concerning Moses, is part of the series of stories concerning the birth of the first human couple and is one of the trials this couple must undergo in the struggle against the god of evil, Ahriman. The fifth and last scene on the left-hand side represents the

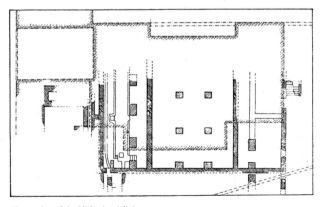

Above: plan of the Mithraic triclinium.
Opposite: fresco representing the story of Mithras.

episode of the *transitus*, as Mithra takes the bull into the cave.

On the right-hand side of the central scene, starting from the bottom, we see Mithra standing and offering a piece of meat (or a drinking horn) to a kneeling figure. The episode probably illustrates the pact of vassalage made between Mithra and the Sun. The next scene shows Mithra with his legs outspread, touching a semicircular line (the vault of heaven). This scene visually sums up the concept according to which Mithra, as the god of light, is also the *mesites*, that is the "dweller of the intermediate zone," since light, brought to us by air, is an intermediary between the sky and Earth. The third scene illustrates Mithra and another figure (almost certainly the Sun) holding two spears in front of an altar, an act that seals the alliance between Mithra and the Sun. The fourth episode shows the Sun standing in his chariot and inviting Mithra to stand beside him. The last scene ends the series with the sacred banquet, in which Mithra and six companions, on a tablinum covered with cushions, carry out the central act of the ritual, which is the conclusion to the god's mythical sacrifice of the bull.

3 – The S. Clemente Mithraeum

Of all the Mithraic caves, the one in San Clemente Church is the most famous because it has a rather complex layout, with four levels that are very different in both character and structure. The lower church of San Clemente, a 4th-century A.D. basilica, was discovered by Father Mullooly and the archaeologist De Rossi, who in 1857 carried out the first exploration and digs and also found a third level under the basilica. This latter was later flooded and was made accessible by Father Nolan only in 1912, when a fourth level was brought to light, consisting of some houses destroyed after Nero's fire in 64 A.D. which, filled with earth, were used as foundations for the new upper edifices.

It was precisely in this fourth level that the Mithraic complex was found: a series of rooms erected in the second half of the 2nd century between the walls of a more ancient *domus*. Among these rooms is the so-called Mithraic School, a rectangular space in which the adepts were most probably instructed before being admitted to the most intimate secrets of the triclinium, or banquet hall. These adepts belonged to the lower levels of initiation, the *Corax*, *Cryphius* (*Nymphus*) and *Miles*, and were not allowed to participate in the Mithraic *agape* or banquet. The room must have had a mosaic pavement with white and black tesserae and a stuccoed vault. The walls have seven niches covered with graffiti related to the seven levels of initiation. One hall (or vestibule) bears signs of what may have been the antechamber and meeting room of the devotees, who sat on the benches all around the room, under a ceiling ornated with geometric and floral motifs.

The pivotal act of the ritual took place in the triclinium, a long and narrow room made oppressive by a low vault dressed with pumice. It is decorated with stucco stars and eleven openings, four of which represent the seasons and the others the seven constellations. The result is a perfect representation of the Mithraic cave. It may be that this decoration aimed at underscoring the presence of the vault of heaven, which is so fraught with symbolism, by having it seem to

Opposite: the marble head in the subterranean basilica narthex.

rotate around the heads of the devotees beneath it. "On the other hand, the cosmos was formed spontaneously and is connatural with matter, which the ancients enigmatically called stone and rock because it seemed to be inert and hostile to form, and they considered it infinite because it was amorphous." (Porphyry). This clarifies the relationship with the cave as well as the allegory of the birth of Mithra, depicted by a small statue set in a fissure in the *specus*, aligned with the altar in the middle of the sanctuary. The young god is emerging upright from the rock, like light from the solid vault of the heavens. In the ancient Indo-Iranian hymns he is in fact described as having "leapt from the rock and gone out of the cave." Along the sides of the room are two long podia and semicircular niches for statues, while in the front end there is a small chamber that seems to have been used as a storeroom for the bones of the sacrificed animals. The chief decorative element in this hall is the central altar, with a representation of the tauroctonia in low relief. The overall treatment of the subject contains the usual elements in this episode: Mithras, the bull, the dog, the scorpion and the serpent. Also present are the inseparable companions of Mithra's retinue, Cautes and Cautopates, the rising and the setting sun, death and life. Together with Mithra, the torchbearers represent the three-fold nature of this divinity.

Above: detail of a sarcophagus with the myth of Hippolytus.
Opposite: the lower basilica, with the remains of the Early Christian pavement at right.

4 – The Mithraeum in the Baths of Caracalla

Beneath the Baths of Caracalla is a maze of passageways and rooms, a network of galleries, *cryptae* and corridors wide enough for the transport of fuel, laundry and everything else needed to maintain and operate the baths. This is a series of chambers in correspondence with the large northwest upper exedra that contain a sanctuary complex.

The first room, which has a small semicircular basin with a barrel vault, leads to another room whose vault has collapsed and which has been identified as the vestibule.

Further on is a marble threshold leading to a large hall with four groin vaults with a large aperture of light at the end. This is a *spelaeum* well constructed behind the somber row of pillars. The two long and side podia that are slightly tapered upward mark off the triclinium area of the sanctuary. A long shelf used for oil-lamps, small torches and other objects employed in the initiation rituals, follows the alignment of the façades. The two podia are not connected to the walls, as there is a passageway between them. Four tiny niches carved out of the podia probably had the same function as those found in San Clemente. In the northwest wall near the corner, a rectangular niche has a fresco with the portrait of a male figure wearing a Phrygian bonnet who can be identified either as Mithra or Cautes or Cautopates. The floor is covered with a mosaic with black and white geometric patterns. The pavement is interrupted by a sunken basin closed with a marble ring that was used for the purification ablutions prescribed in the ritual. This basin was considered a demoniacal imitation of baptism by the Church Fathers, and in particular by Tertullian, who inveighed against it in no uncertain terms, stating that "even those devoid of all intellectual interest in the divine powers, believe their idols have the same efficacy [as baptism], but they deceive themselves with sterile water."

Another opening lies in the pavement. This is a deep hole connected to a passageway leading to the adjacent rooms used as an *apparitorium* (dressing room). This may have been one of the many means of

Opposite: passageway between the Mithraeum vestibule and the apparitorium.

transporting the sacrificed bull, or a way of enhancing the theatrical elements of the initiation trials, much like a proscenium. What is certain is that the access to the service rooms, directly connected underground with the pit in the main hall, evokes the *taurobolium* rite, the gruesome ablutions with the blood of the sacrificed bull. Just as in the *Magna Mater* ritual, it seems that the devotees of the Iranian god also took part in that grisly baptism, having themselves lowered into those pits–also known as *fassae sanguinis*, or bloody pits–where the blood of the bull poured onto them from above would, they believed, cleanse them of their impurities. Before the ritual entered its most crucial stage, many other acts had to be carried out. Many rooms were used an an *apparitorium* for this purpose: here the adepts dressed and undressed, or put the sacred objects after they had been used in ceremonies. This room, with a low ledge on the back wall supported by four small vaults, was certainly conceived with this purpose in mind and was connected to the main hall via the above-mentioned passageway. Two square rooms flanking this passageway were most certainly latrines, since one

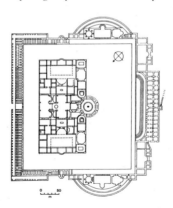

0   50
m

Above: plan of the Baths of Caracalla.
Opposite: the back wall of the triclinium.

is connected to a sewer and in the other the waste was dropped down a small hole.

The entire complex must have been richly decorated. Proof of this is the discovery of a headless statue of Venus in the *spelunca magna*. But why should a Venus be in a Mithraic sanctuary? It is known that some inscriptions referring to the cult of Mithra mention Venus Genetrix. Also, there are some bas-reliefs which, like imitations of Praxiteles' sculpture of the goddess of beauty and love, depict the goddess twisting her hair while looking into a mirror. It is difficult to determine where the statue was placed, but archaeologists think it stood with the other statues that decorated the apse at the end of the room, which is now illuminated by a fascinating shaft of light. In reality, upon entering, the adepts would have found themselves in a dark, damp and oppressive atmosphere, the expression of that underground world the Christians scornfully referred to as *castra tenebrarum*.

Death

The Manes and the Cult of the Dead

The Manes were the spirits of the dead, supernatural beings who could be repudiated or propitiated and who, according to ancient Roman tradition, wandered around the homes of their relatives, somewhat like the family ghosts. If properly propitiated they could come to the aid of their descendants, but if neglected they might turn out to be quite harmful and vindictive and could even take on the grim appearance of *lemures* or *larvae*, thus disturbing the peace and quiet of the living, as Plautus tells us: "[...] he says that the dead man had appeared to him in a dream." In order to ward off fear, the ancient Romans relied on special formulas and rites that Ovid describes in almost pedantic detail: "At midnight, when silence invites sleep, / and you hold your peace, oh dogs and multicoloured birds, / he who recalls the ancient rite and is in awe of the gods / leaps out of bed without putting sandals on his feet / and snaps his fingers with his thumb and middle finger / in order not to meet a shadowy spirit, and remains silent. / After purifying his hands in the waters of the spring, / he turns and first puts black beans in his mouth; / then he casts them behind his shoulders while uttering: / 'I throw them and deliver myself and my relatives from harm's way with these beans!' / Nine times he says this, nor does he look behind him. He believes /that the spirit gathers them up and follows him unseen. / Again he purifies his hands, strikes the bronze bells of Temesa / and prays that that spirit

Opposite: the columbaria of Vigna Codini.

leave his house. / 'Spirits of our ancestors, go out' he repeats nine times; / he turns and believes the ritual has been performed with purity."

This was an individual ritual to placate the lonely, hungry spirits and exorcise fear of the presence of the *lemures* or the evil and dangerous *larvae*. The entire ritual was performed with the utmost deference and care: the ritual cleansing with pure spring water, the use of black beans, the striking of the bells. What with the constant repetition of the formulas and Ovid's lively narration, it seems as if we could almost catch a glimpse of the spirits emerging from the darkness by following the various ritual acts one after the other. The Manes spirits were invoked in almost all the inscriptions with the traditional formula *D(is) M(anibus)* or *D(is) M(anibus) S(acrum)*, followed by the name or names of the deceased.

The ancient Romans' veneration of the dead was part of a tradition of respect for the memory of their dead relatives and was also partly due to the superstitions mentioned above. There were many public manifestations of the cult of the dead, and quite a few private ones as well, such as the *dies natalis* (the deceased's birthday). One of the major ceremonies was the official commemoration of the deceased, the *Parentalia* or *dies Parentales*, which were held on February 13-21 (the last day–known as the *Feralia*–was reserved for public ceremonies, while the others were dedicated to the private family ones). Whether they were *Feralia*, *Lemuria* or *Parentalia*, on all these occasions devout attention was paid to the mortal remains in their tombs and to ensuring them comfort and rest. This ranged from the simplest food offerings–bread and grapes–to sweets and sausages and even to banquets with guests (*epulae*), an act in which the living shared food with the dead. There was no lack of incense, fruit and flowers of all kinds, especially violets and roses, which were considered guarantees of eternal spring in the afterlife: "Sprinkle wine and perfumed oil on my ashes, / oh guest, and add balsam to the red roses. / My unmourned urn enjoys perpetual spring. / I am not dead, I have only changed worlds." (Ausonius).

Funerary Rites

The funeral (*funus*) and the period preceding it involved a complex ritual, and there were major differences according to the economic and social status of the deceased. The richer he had been, or the more public or military offices he had held, the more solemn and complex was his funeral ceremony (*funus publicum*, *funus militare* or *funus imperatorium*). The *pater familias* (or his heir, should he himself be the deceased) was responsible for organizing the ceremony. First of all, the deceased was kissed (since the soul was believed to leave the body from the mouth), then his name was repeated aloud three times as a farewell (*conclamatio*), after which specialized persons (*libitinarii*) washed and scented the corpse with perfumed oils and other potions. After the corpse was dressed, it was placed in the atrium of the house, its feet facing the front door. It lay there on display for several days, so that strongly scented essences (candles, boxes of incense and flowers) were scattered over the vestibule to cover the smell of the decomposing body. When necessary, a form of embalming was adopted to delay the unpleasant effects of decomposition. A coin was often placed in the mouth of the deceased; this was an *obulus Carontis*, a sort of tax for ferrying the dead from the Earth to Hades. If the deceased was an adult male of noble rank, his portrait—in conformity with precise legal regula-

White stucco tondo in the burial chamber of the Tomb of the Valerii.

tions (*ius imaginum*)–was allowed to be displayed in the form of a wax death mask (*imago*) that reproduced his facial features. "The image is a wax mask that closely resembles the deceased in both appearance and complexion," says Polybius in his *Historiae*. "During the public sacrifices, the Romans display these images and honour them solemnly. And when some other illustrious member of the family dies, these images participate in the ceremony by covering persons similar in height and shape to the deceased to whom they first belonged. If the deceased was a consul or strategus, he is dressed in garments bordered in scarlet; if he was a censor, purple togas; if he earned a triumph or some similar honour, robes embroidered with gold. Thus adorned, they proceed on carts, and before them are carried fasces, axes and the other emblems that usually accompany magistrates, in keeping with the honours that each received from the state during his lifetime. Once the procession has arrived at the Rostra, everyone sits in order on ivory seats. A young man who loves honour and virtue could hardly wish to witness a more beautiful sight. In fact, who would not be urged to emulation upon seeing, all together, the images of men who are distinguished for their virtues, as if they were alive and breathing? What could be more beautiful than such a spectacle?" Therefore, the funeral ceremony was often a lavish display that made use of theatrical representations with a strong emotional impact. The funeral procession began with the corpse on a litter (*sandapila*). This was followed by the close relatives dressed in black and by a group of women, professional mourners (*praeficae*) whose weeping was a dramatic manifestation of the entire family's grief. Sometimes they had receptacles hanging under their eyes in which their tears dropped, thus serving as proof of the authenticity of their performance. The ceremony also included musicians, mimes and dancers who–in the case of illustrious persons–accompanied the procession as far as the Forum, where, on the Rostra, the ceremony ended with the funerary oration.

The Tombs

The attention paid to ritual and to the funeral ceremony helps to explain the genesis of the tombs and how they were arranged. From the earliest type, the burial of ashes, to interment, from the simplest stela to monumental and elaborate forms of the mausoleum, Roman tombs reveal an attachment to the reality of life and the yearning to overcome death through the memory of the living. The prevailing concept was that of the deceased in close contact with the living and with the members of his family and his *gens*. The central idea in this respect could therefore be summed up in the saying *non omnis morior* (I will not be wholly dead). This ideal contact and dialogue between the dead and the living is manifested in the very location of the cemeteries, which, given the desire to be exposed to the view of the living, were placed along the sides of the main avenues rather than in more densely populated areas in the city. Again, the almost tangible presence of the deceased through their statues and the detailed description of their deeds, is further confirmation of the continuous dialogue with the living. Indeed, there were even some cases in which the inscriptions directly addressed the passers-by. It is difficult to provide a chronology of the architectural styles of the tombs. Although in some cases the choice of a funerary monument in ancient Roman society was a question of fashion, it was basically determined by the economic resources of the patron as well as his social and political role in society, and its formal and decorative elements expressed his ideals.

Monte del Grano, detail of the sarcophagus lid.

5 – The Tombs along the Via Latina

A stretch of the Roman countryside saved from the invasion of cement has retained the fascination of an ancient road flanked by trees and tombs. Here, at the 4th milestone of the Via Latina, among the rows of evergreen trees and tombs, one's taste and passion for the past will be revived. This stone-paved road leads to a solitary rural area far from the chaotic traffic of Rome, evoking the past with its funerary monuments. The first interesting architectural work is the tall and stately Barberini tomb, whose most distinguishing aesthetic feature is the elegantly patterned brickwork in two colours. With its sober, orderly lines, it is modelled after the small temples that were so popular during the Antonine period. The upper floor, which was reached via an internal staircase, was richly decorated with frescoes and painted stuccowork on the vault that became blackened by centuries of use as a shelter by farmers and shepherds.

The next monument is the Tomb of the Valerii, whose well-preserved exterior may very well mislead visitors into thinking it is the original structure, while it is really the result of a very free interpretation on the part of 19th-century restorers. However, the underground approach, introduced by an atrium, more than makes up for our initial disappointment. In fact, the entrance is like a white, mystical world of stuccowork: Tritons, Nereids, griffons and sea monsters mingle with cupids and dancing maenads to form a geometric pattern of squares and circles on the ceiling. It is no easy task to unravel the symbolic meaning of these figures, and the viewer ends up enjoying a happy, radiant representation of the underworld, a sort of endless dance dedicated to the passage to the empyrean. In the central medallion, a flying griffon is taking a soul to the afterlife.

The spiritual substance of the deceased therefore becomes a tangible female image and reconstructs and clarifies the overall meaning of this figurative tumult, translating this system of

Opposite: white stucco decoration on the vault of the Tomb of the Valerii.

eternal beatitude into a clear-cut, essential apotheosis, the geometric and harmonious rhythm of which is broken only by the allusive and temporal admonition of the Hours.

The Tomb of the Pancratii also surprises visitors. It is an underground chamber that is reached via the original stairway, preceded by a vestibule with a lovely brick bench on its side supported by small arches. A row of sarcophagi must once have lain on that ledge, which is now mostly empty except for one fluted sarcophagus with the image of the deceased in a decorative medallion. In the innermost chamber is an enormous sarcophagus that tells us nothing either about its age or owner. First distracted by its sheer massiveness, we are then utterly dazzled

Above: Tomb of the Pancratii, the vestibule of the burial chamber.
Opposite: the Tomb of the Pancratii.

by the splendid, radiant vault decoration: a symphony of colour, with ochre, carmine and purple stuccowork and frescoes depicting myths. Griffons, candelabra, lions and centaurs on the whitish plaster frame the principal scenes. There is Admetus, accompanied by Apollo and Diana, who triumphantly shows Pelias the cart drawn by harnessed animals; Priam before Achilles to ask for the body of his son Hector; a determined Paris choosing the most beautiful of the three goddesses; and lastly, Hercules being received on Mt. Olympus. The gods and immortal heroes in these scenes are marked out by the ineluctable force of Fate, which watches over this universe of stucco and painting, as well as the lives and acts of men.

6 – Monte del Grano

The scene is a square in the city outskirts like so many others, with deafening traffic and blocks and blocks of ugly buildings, all alike. The only exception is a hillock crowned by olive trees that with its fresh greenery injects some brightness into that otherwise dull and depressing area of cement. However, the inhabitants of this quarter do not seem to be aware of the ancient relic amid the liveliness and noise of the marketplace. And in fact, there is nothing here that suggests its man-made interior, not even its name–Monte del Grano, or Mount of Grain–which, on the contrary, would seem to indicate a purely natural setting.

According to a local legend, this hill grew out of a huge pile of grain that was gathered there on a holiday and was therefore subject to divine punishment, destroyed and transformed into earth by a bolt of lightning. But it is really a majestic tumulus whose inverted cone shape, which closely resembles a modius (a unit of grain measure in ancient Rome: *modium grani*) gave rise to its name in corrupted form, as a medieval document tells us: "et cum parte Modii sive Montanis vel Montis dello Grano."

The rich stepped travertine decoration on the exterior that characterized this mound tomb has completely disappeared. It was removed in 1387 by Nicolò Valentini, the owner of the site, in order to "excavate, extract and break all the existing travertine both within and without the mound known as Monte del Grano," and above all "transport it elsewhere and transform it into good, utilizable lime."

In the 16th century the monument, which by then had lost its marble dressing, had acquired a tower which was restored by Lovatti in 1870 and then collapsed during a gale. In the late 20th century a splendid 3rd-century A.D. sarcophagus was discovered inside which was erroneously believed to belong to the emperor Alexander Severus and his mother Julia Mamaea. "I remember, outside San Giovanni Gate, a mile past the aqueducts, at the place called Monte del Grano,

Opposite: gallery leading to the round chamber.

there was a large ancient mass of rubble. It was not difficult for a quarryman to break into it and go inside by letting himself down so far that he found a large figured sarcophagus with the Rape of the Sabine Women and, on the lid, two reclining figures with the features of Alexander Severus and Julia Mamaea, his mother, while inside were their ashes. At present this tomb is to be found at the Campidoglio, in the middle of the courtyard of the Palazzo dei Conservatori." (Flaminio Vacca).

Actually, the narration carved on the sarcophagus has nothing to do with Alexander Severus and his mother Mamaea, but are scenes from the life of Achilles: but this does not explain why this tomb-mausoleum was for so long considered that of the last of the Severus emperors. Some scholars think the sarcophagus had contained one of the most highly prized examples of glass-cameo art, the famous Portland Vase

Cross section of the Monte del Grano mound.

(late 1st century A.D.), which is justly famous for its splendid classic style decoration executed with such great skill. The masterful carving of this magnificent piece is eloquent proof of the refined taste of the art patrons in that age and their desire to possess rare and precious objects. A small gate hidden in the surrounding garden opens into the vast circular hall, which is the interior of this ancient tumulus, whose bare, rough structure is now covered with a thick layer of hardened earth. The utter darkness and oppressive and damp atmosphere make it difficult to imagine the luxuriousness of the original mausoleum, its sumptuous decoration, which included a beautiful ring of marble columns. We must therefore use Piranesi's imaginative engraving of the tomb to reconstruct it in our mind and put that commonplace hillock in the outskirts of Rome in its rightful place as an outstanding monument.

The Monte del Grano dome.

7 – The Necropolis along the Via Ostiense

Not far from St. Paul's Basilica is a group of tombs and columbaria dating from the early years of the Roman Republic to the late Imperial Age. Behind the enclosure fence is a jumble of recesses, aedicules, sarcophagi and chests, a meandering course among the mortal remains of slaves and freedmen who left their last message to the living from these burial sites. They introduce themselves with their family names, age and occupation, and invoke the Manes spirits of the dead to help them in the passage to the afterlife. The tombs lie along alleys and narrow streets and have a certain architectural dignity about them, with touches of extreme elegance. Be they individual or guild tombs, they proudly exhibit their epigraphs, and the delicately rendered paintings evoke the state of bliss of the other world.

In the northern section of the necropolis, the most ancient tombs have tufa façades and are flanked by other Imperial Age brick tombs. In the small chamber below the stairway on the side, a peacock is strutting ostentatiously, and next to it a muscular Hercules is saving Alcestes from the grip of Hades. This scene is in a small painted recess hidden among the tombs in the shadow of a stairway, but the darkness in no way detracts from the proud declaration of triumph over death. Not far away is a large early Imperial Age burial area with *opus recticulatum* masonry. Lying against the enclosure wall are sepulchres dating from different periods that were placed there to save space. Two niche tombs, one in marble and the other made of bricks, do not manage to make up for the rather poor quality of the others, which are nothing more than mere pits or earth graves.

On the opposite side are two rectangular areas whose walls dotted with recesses clearly show they were used as columbaria. The first, the one closer to the entrance, has an elegant aedicule whose façade, framed by garlands of daisies, has a painting of two lionesses attacking a gazelle. Next to this is a small well with traces of a dolium mouth. The funerary vessels with inscriptions that were

Opposite: the niches of the gens Pontia columbarium *(1st century A.D.).*

found here belong to the *gens Pontia* (1st century A.D.).

Other interesting columbaria (1st century A.D.) stand on a lane that intersects with the Via Ostiense, their small brick façades, originally crowned by a triangular tympanum, aligned in a row. One in particular is striking: the columbarium of Livia Nebris, daughter of Marcus, who is buried here with other members of the family. Delicate festoons and floral motifs cover the walls filled with many recesses, lending a festive air to the interior. The outer travertine jamb gives us the size with pedantic precision: *in fr(onte) p(edes) VI* (width) and *in ag(ro) p(edes) VIII* (length). Next to it, an irregularly shaped room surrounded by pit graves has been identified as the seat of the college or family (*schola*) that had built the graves for its members. Now one can barely make out a series of painted panels with flying figures. For the most part they are birds that seem to be soaring in the white background as if they were lost in the vastness of space. Among the griffons and winged horses, only the eagle on the globe seems to be at ease in that infinite domain that lives only in Man's imagination.

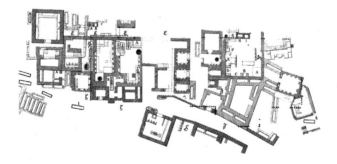

Above: plan of the funerary complex.

Opposite, above: fresco of the columbaria on a lane facing the Via Ostiense; below: a tomb in the necropolis.

8 – The Mausoleum of Romulus

Facing the *carceres* of the Circus of Maxentius and partly hidden by a large country house, the tomb of Romulus embodies the lavishness of imperial residences in late antiquity. It was part of a residential complex laid out to celebrate the grandeur of the emperor and his *gens*, modelled after the new encomiastic parameters imported from the East, in which villa, circus and mausoleum together were in keeping with the political and architectural ideology that prevailed in the 4th century. This consisted in glorifying the quasi-divine role of the emperor, who during his lifetime was acclaimed in the circus and after his death was deified in the mausoleum. This latter stood in the middle of a quadriporticus with brick arcades at the second milestone of the Appian Way. A round structure, much like the Pantheon in its majestic solemnity, it was meant to be a eulogy of Romulus, the emperor Maxentius' young son who died prematurely in 309 A.D. at the age of nine.

"This edifice lies outside Rome near San Sebastiano and is in a state of total ruin, especially the loggias around it. But the central building,

Above: fresco on the back wall of the vestibule.
Opposite: view of the round tambour of the mausoleum with the central pier.

being solidly constructed, is perfectly intact. It is made of bricks, with no ornament of any kind, and it is gloomy because it has no other light than that from the door and the four niches like tiny windows [...]; the part indicated is barrel-vaulted and the middle section is a pier as solid as bedrock that supports said vault, in the middle of which is an opening. The central pier is ornated with niches like those in the wall." Sebastiano Serlio (1475-1554) was the first person to give a detailed description of the mausoleum, but other architects, from Sangallo to Palladio and Canina, made studies and reconstructions.

Today nothing remains of the structure above ground, and one can only imagine its original size from the vast proportions. What is left are the underground chambers, which with their cylindrical tambour reach the level of the floor of the cella above, which was used as a large terrace, a sort of circular hanging garden, by the owners of the country house. One enters this latter via the remains of the ancient access stairway, which replaced the original hexastyle pronaos that gave the monument a sanctuary-like aspect when viewed from the front. It was once possible to go from here into the cella, a round space surrounded by niches and columns and with a large vault that opened to the sky through a large central oculus, much like the one in the Pantheon.

A stairway leads to the interior, a sort of vestibule whose rough walls are barely animated by ancient graffiti and a few frescoes from a later period. The gloomy atmosphere is a prelude to the innermost hall, the heart of Romulus' tomb. An ambulatory winds around the funerary sacrarium. The enormous central pier seems to keep the vault suspended over the ambulatory; the patterns of the alternating semicircular and rectangular niches on the pier, repeated on the wall opposite it, mark the rhythm of this room.

Rays of light penetrating through the small openings attenuate the darkness of the monument. In fact, the entire architectural structure is dominated by the idea of a cave, and not even the smoothly plastered walls manage to dispel the fascination of the *spelunca*. Despite the vaulted ceiling and the niches, which create an artificial atmo-sphere, the ambulatory emanates a mysterious dimension that lies halfway between the natural and the artificial.

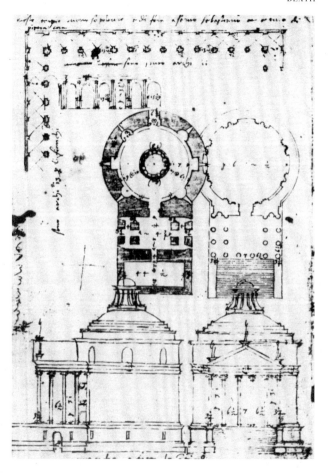

Plan and elevation of the Mausoleum of Romulus (drawing by Palladio).

9 – The Mausoleum of Lucilius Peto

The round profile of the mausoleum of Lucilius Peto emerges from a hollow along the ancient salt road (Via Salaria). Like so many Etruscan tumuli, it exudes majesty and noble dignity, a tribute to the memory of those who found their final resting place here. An inscription tells us that it belonged to two wealthy members of the *gens Lucilia*, Lucilius Peto, a military tribune and prefect of the blacksmiths and the cavalry, and his sister Lucilia Polla. The epigraph, carved on a marble slab, is in the middle of the round tambour and is surrounded by a casing of smooth travertine ashlars to form a compact, geometric pattern above a cornice. Above this simple, sober design is a green conical mound of earth. This is a round tomb, a type much in fashion during Augustus' age that can be dated from the late 1st century A.D.

An arched door opens onto a long corridor, a narrow *dromos* with a plastered vault. On the walls are two rows of loculi, some of which

still have the large tiles or pieces of marble used to seal them, which shows that this corridor was used as a catacomb in a relatively late period. Most of these recesses are small, so they were most probably used for children.

The dark corridor leads to the cruciform cella, which has three niches. Four ledge-like protuberances in the corners of the walls served as pillars, supporting the weight of the vault, and the niches clearly reveal they were used to house a *kline*, or funerary bed. The rudimental stairway leads to the entrance, where the walls with their numerous loculi reveal this was a true catacomb ambulatory hewn out of the tufa, most probably in the first centuries of the Christian era, perhaps by the descendants of the family that had commissioned the mausoleum, who may have converted to Christianity.

The embedded marble mound lies in a depression.

10 – The S. Sebastiano Mausoleums

The labyrinth of underground passageways between the 3rd and 2nd milestones of the Appian Way clearly reveals radical changes in the notions of funerary rituals and the afterlife. The tradition of the *memoria apostolorum* connected to the cult of Saints Peter and Paul, which at a later date was associated with the martyr St. Sebastian, may lead people to believe that this block of sandstone with its many carved loculi was used exclusively by catechumens and *fossores*, or gravediggers. Then one realizes that this was in fact a catacomb, that is, an area which acquired its name from the fact that it lay near a cave (*katà kymbas* in Greek means "near the cavity"). This subterranean site offers visitors a highly refined spectacle that is quite a different thing from the gloomy series of catacombs described by Goethe: "The visit to the catacombs, on the other hand, did not come up to my expectations; my first steps in those sad underground vaults aroused such restlessness in me that I immediately went back up to see the sun again and to wait, in that otherwise secluded and neglected district, for my travelling companions who, less impressionable than I, were able to visit even those places in utter tranquillity."

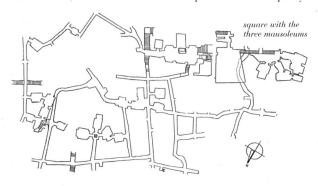

square with the three mausoleums

Above: plan of the S. Sebastiano subterranean areas.
Opposite: the funerary square with the three small mausoleums.

The most ancient documentation of this monument dates from the end of the Roman Republic and consists of a suburban villa that originally stood on an alley parellel to the Appian Way. Another smaller villa, together with some columbaria, are the result of later construction.

These are not the only pagan structures here. The succession of periods and centuries witnessed the construction of an unusual and interesting small cemetery which, after a drastic change made in the 2nd century, was the result of earth filling that elevated the original level of the floor (nine metres below the church pavement) by more than three metres. Here there are three small sarcophagi with their fronts still intact, and a burial chamber covered with frescoes and stuccowork. As can be seen in the inscription, the mausoleums belonged to M(arcus) Clodius Hermes, the *Innocentiores* association, and the *Ascia*, named after an axe carved on the façade. These elegant mausoleums were certainly pagan and date from the end of Hadrian's rule.

The first at right, Hermes' mausoleum, paradoxically looks like a hymn to spring and to life. The frescoes on the plastered walls depict baskets brimming with fruit, flowers and birds soaring through an eternal garden of delights created to soothe the soul of the deceased in a symbolic paradise. "I want fruit of all kinds, flowers and birds, and wine in abundance around my ashes," says Trimalchio in a famous passage in Petronius Arbiter's *Satirycon*. All around, amid the blood-red octagonal decoration, there must have been the representation of the funeral rite: from the oration in honour of the deceased to the leave-taking of his wife, friends and relatives. In the middle of the vault is a Gorgon's mask that would seem to disturb that soave otherworldly dance, if it were not for its apotropaic function of refuge and protection.

The second mausoleum, called *Innocentiores*, is dressed with geometric stuccowork that culminates in the augural embrace of a peacock, a symbol of immortality.

The third mausoleum, which like the others is two storeys high, has a carved axe symbolizing both a work tool and the inviolability of the tomb. Like the preceding mausoleum, its vault is decorated with stuccoed circles and rosettes–an extremely elegant work that calls the attention of the living to their own tombs.

Top: detail of the lunette above the arcosolium.
Above: the Mausoleum of Marcus Clodius Hermes.

11 – The Pyramid

With their steep upward thrust, pyramids have always embodied the idea of a path to the heavens for the soul on its journey to its celestial abode. This is the reason why with time the pyramid has become the symbol of the funerary monument. The fascination of its perfect geometrical form, its grandeur, its abstract linearity, have made it the archetype of man's striving for the infinite.

The earliest examples were step pyramids (such as the one at Saqqara). Only in a later period, in order to avoid the inconvenience of the continuous deposit of rubble and sand carried by the wind, did the ancient Egyptians decide to dress the pyramids and make their surfaces smooth. The symbolism of the stairway to the sky was thus transformed into the precise and austere geometry of the pyramid proper. Perhaps its construction was inspired by sun worship, by the concept of the monolith crowned by this radiant star.

Drawing inspiration from the Eyptian models, four pyramids were built in ancient Rome during the Augustan period, only one of which has survived: the pyramid of Caius Cestius, which for the Romans represented the entire category. There were also the twin pyramids in the Campus Martius, positioned much like propylaea at the entrance to the Via Lata, where Bernini's churches, Santa Maria in Monesanto and Santa Maria dei Miracoli, now stand; and another pyramid, known as the Borgo pyramid, stood near St. Peter's and was destroyed by Pope Alexander VI to make room for a new road he had laid out in the Borgo. Medieval legends associated this latter pyramid with Romulus, calling it *Meta Romuli*, which was coupled with the Cestius pyramid, which was thought to be the *Meta Remi*. "In the middle of the wall was built / a large tomb of great dimensions / where Romulus was buried after his death." This erroneous attribution from a 15th-century source must not have lasted long, since Poggio Bracciolini correctly transcribed the name, which appears on the inscription on the façade: C(AIUS) CESTIUS L(UCI) F(ILIUS) EPULO,

Opposite: the Pyramid of Cauius Cestius seen from the cemetery.

POB(lilia tribu), PRAETOR, TRIBUNUS PLEBIS (septem) VIR EPULORUM. Thus, sometime between 18 and 12 B.C., Caius Cestius, the septem-vir of the epulones–that is, a priest in the prestigious college in charge of organizing ritual sacrificial banquets for the gods (*epulae*)–decided to depart from the traditional style of tombs and propose a clearly Oriental-inspired model. He thus built his stairway to the sky on a large travertine podium, dressing it with blocks of white marble.

Situated at the crossroads of two major ancient roads, the *Ostiensis* and the *Vicus Portac Raudusculunae*, the pyramid now solemnly dominates the sky of the Testaccio district. Enclosed by the Aurelian walls, its vertical cusp reminds one of the "Egyptian" fashion of the time, and the compact white surface invites one to search for a threshold, an entrance. Once past the small door, one can hardly adjust to the difference between the sudden darkness here and the brightness outside. The long, narrow corridor is like a sort of preparation, almost a

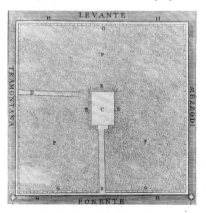

Above: plan of the pyramid (engraving by Piranesi).

Opposite: a Piranesi engraving of the monument in the 18th century.

cathartic journey to the final destination, the burial chamber, where everything seems so small compared to the massive walls above it. However, the small size in no way detracts from its fascination, but actually increases it. One's feeling of disorientation vanishes in front of the row of female figures painted on the walls. They are reading, carrying lustral water jars or holding long tibiae, emerging from the worn-out plaster to watch over the deceased with the serene and delicate grace of Third Style paintings. Surrounded by candelabra, vases and grotesques, these figures, so aloof and a trifle haughty in their rich robes, appear to be recoiling from the glances of modern visitors. On the vault, these figures are lighter, more ethereal in the guise of Victories sustaining the final apotheosis of Caius Cestius. Unfortunately, these scenes are known only through old engravings and 18th-century drawings, since the ravages of time have reduced the elegant composition to a few rather indistinct figures.

Columbaria

Columbaria began to be used on a large scale in Rome during the Augustan age, when a new type of collective burial was created by funerary associations to meet the needs of the growing population. The origin of the columbarium is uncertain. The word dervies from the Latin *columba*, or dove, because the walls with their niches looked like dovecotes. Each niche, or loculus, could house even two or three cinerary urns, which allowed for hundreds and hundreds of burials in a relatively small space. The system called for cremation, after which the deceased's ashes were placed in clay jars or in urns made of alabaster, marble or even metal. On the outer edge of the bottom of the niche was the name of the deceased, and the wall around it was decorated with ornamental motifs and small genre or mythological scenes. In general, these columbaria were small and well-built in every detail with taste and elegance–much like a miniature funerary chest in which small niches with columns and pediments merge the architectural elements in a variegated whole of great decorative impact. The columbaria often belonged to rather modest funeral corporations or to freed slaves of patrician Roman families. Since individual tombs were out of the question because of their high cost, these people got together in associations that would guarantee their ashes would be placed in modest but decent burial sites. Naturally, for well-off persons the tombs were richer and more elaborate: the columbaria were decorated with stuccowork and paintings and contained niches beautified by slender figurines in which theosophical and transcendental concepts were expressed metaphorically. One recurring motif is that of festive nature abounding in flowers and fruit and with birds and cupids flying overhead.

The act of burial was meant to give the body back to the earth from which it was born, whereas cremation corresponded to the Neo-Platonic concept whereby the soul was freed from its "terrestrial prison," the body.

Opposite: the apse at the end of Pomponius Hylas' columbarium.

12 – The Columbarium of Pomponius Hylas

In an isolated part of the Parco degli Scipioni, this small house passes
unnoticed. But once we go over the threshold and onto the steep stairway, all memory of the present is left behind, and we find a different
dimension of death.

The first thing we see is a clear warning not to disturb this site. Along
the stairs, in the front wall, two facing griffons in front of a cithara
keep guard over the mosaic inscription which indicates that this is the
entrance. In reality, they are apotropaic figures meant to ward off evil.
Brilliant glass tesserae tell us the names of those who may have been the
owners of the tomb, Pomponius Hylas and his wife Pomponia Vitalinis:
CN(aei). POMPONI HILAE (et) POMPONIAE. CN(aei). L(ibertae) VITALINIS.

A surprise is in store for us at the foot of the stairs. Rather than a dark,
gloomy sepulchre, it is a delicately and exquisitely wrought sacellum, at
once intimate and lively: the colourful background is truly enchanting
and the alternating rhythm of the frontals attracts our attention to the
salient points. Thus we discover figures and stories amid the pattern of
blood reds, burnt earth and ultramarine blues.

Recesses resembling small sanctuaries divide the walls of this cham-

Above: detail of the mosaic on the wall facing the access stairway.
Opposite: the alternating rhythm of the frontals is clearly seen here.

ber, and in this case the name "columbarium" is wholly inadequate. It is more like a theatre, neither tragic nor comic, but rather a theatre for the sweet music of the afterlife.

In the small triangular space of the pediment in front of the stairway, a stucco figure of Chiron is teaching Achilles to play the lyre, thus extolling the cathartic role of music in a serene representation of the Elysian Fields. Below this, in the frieze on the architrave, Ocnus is twirling his rope, in company with the three-headed Cerberus and a fleeing Danaid; this is probably an allusion to the tribulations of Tartarus, the underworld. Redemption is celebrated on the vault in the dance of the cupids among a labyrinth of grapevines: one is unrolling a papyrus scroll, another is trying to walk on a branch, and the third one, absorbed in reading, is apparently oblivious of the one next to him swinging from a tendril. This fresco is a minuet of cupids and birds that relieves us of the oppressive weight of that earthen vault overhead and reveals a new, infinite dimension.

Above: stucco of the centaur Chiron teaching Achilles to play the lyre.
Opposite: marble plaque indicating the name, age and family of the deceased.

The composition is dominated by Orpheus. On the central pediment, standing out against the light blue background, he is in the guise of *Iacchos*, while he appears with his usual features in the frieze below, where he seems to be ending his earthly existence in the Dionysian frenzy of the Bacchantes. This story, represented in several episodes, is apparently an invitation not to reveal the Orphic mysteries, not to unravel the enigma of the myth contained in his mystical cist. The figures of the two patrons, the two deceased depicted in the middle of the alcove, seem to be indicating the road to take and inviting us to follow it. And in view of their expression of farewell and, above all, their profession of Orphic faith, it is irrelevant whether these figures are identified as Pomponius Hylas and his wife or Granius Nestor with his wife Vinileia Hedone. Everything seems to be revealed allegorically, conveying a message of belief and participation in the Orphic mysteries, and the *Nikai* suspended from the vault also announce the victory over death and eternal salvation.

13 – The Columbaria of Vigna Codini

Behind the Porta Latina, among the well-protected, elegant villas in this area, there are three major columbaria whose roofs can be seen above the ground. Nothing remains of this legacy of the past except for the columbaria of Vigna Codini, which were found in the first half of the 19th century by Marchese Campana and Pietro Codini, who owned the land. These are three subterranean burial complexes dating from Tiberius' or Nero's period.

The first columbarium, which has a large square chamber below ground level, is rather disturbing. An enormous central pier filled with niches supports the weight of the massive vault. A steep stairway leads down to the interior, which contains the arched funerary loculi arranged in nine superimposed rows. Two other rows of clay vessels wind around the lower part of the chamber wall. The atmosphere is rather oppressive in that funerary passageway filled with empty niches which were the last home of so many married couples' ashes. The chamber was decorated with lively figures, multicoloured birds and flowers. This was no mere ornamentation, but rather an attempt to accompany the deceased with elegant representations of the celestial garden: behind those images lies a need for spiritual elevation and redemption.

The second columbarium is a large cube pierced with niches and with a floor made of *opus signinum* masonry. Here again the lower section of the wall with niches was occupied by painted or marble plaques bearing the names of the deceased, who were freed slaves from the imperial court. They had built this collective burial site at their own expense and had also seen to its decoration, placing around the recesses many miniature monuments with architectural niches supported by columns or pilasters in coloured marble or stucco. Around the niches they had frescoes painted with lively motifs entwined by plants and accompanied by Dionysian cymbals, cists and drinking horns in an attempt to flee from the gloomy aura of death.

The third columbarium, which is larger and more majestic, is distin-

Opposite: the huge central pier in the first columbarium has numerous niches.

guished by its original U-shape with three communicating arms. A double stairway leads to the interior, which was probably decorated throughout with frescoes on the vaults and walls divided by pilasters with coloured marble capitals. Today an idea of the effect the original decoration must have made can be gained from the small fragments that have survived on the vault and between the niches. The spaces between the loculi, mostly dressed in marble, are square so as to make room for the cinerary urns, while the inscriptions tell us they belonged to slaves and freed slaves of the imperial house. The chamber is filled with inscriptions that seem to speak to us; besides the usual invocations to the Manes spirits of the dead, they have the names, age and social status of the deceased. One epigraph is a blunt, stern warning: "*Ne tangito, o mortalis, revere Mane deos!*" (Do not touch, oh mortal being, respect the Manes!).

Above: the third columbarium.
Opposite: the second columbarium is a large square chamber with several niches.

Water

A nymphaeum is a room or temple sacred to nymphs. Whether they are Nereids, Naiads or Oceanids, nymphs govern the clear waters of springs and fountains, ensuring their vital and procreative flow: "Fountains and brooks belong to water nymphs." And according to Homer they are the daughters of Zeus, lovely maidens frequently found in clearings and woods, where they are free to indulge in their favourite activities, hunting or dancing in the meadows. They generate and raise heroes, live in caves, in damp places where water flows, interpreting the magical qualities, sounds and force emanating from this element. Nymphs embrace all the manifestations of Nature as personifications of the emotion produced by contemplating it. These young and graceful creatures embody the reactions of the soul at the sight of the attractions and delights of Nature. And they animate the emotional impact made by gazing upon simple natural scenery: in peaceful isolated valleys, in the recesses of cool woods or in the fascinating solitude of the banks in bloom beside babbling streams. Enchanting and alluring, they are dangerous for those who are seduced by the excessive emotions they stimulate. It was said that anyone who caught sight of a nymph would go mad. This is why the mentally disturbed were usually thought to be possessed by nymphs. Madness, "overwhelming rapture," was the outcome of being kidnapped by a nymph. A later superstition speaks of the insanity that strikes those who, affected by an ambivalent feeling of

Opposite: detail of the decoration in the nymphaeum of the Annibaldi.

fear and attraction, catch a glimpse of a figure emerging from water. If nymphs represent the many manifestations of Nature, the ancient Greeks typified them through water and its dual symbolism. Water was considered a purifying wellspring of life that contained all its seeds. This is the reason why nymphs are associated with marriage and, in particular, the bridal bath. The custom of brides going to the local river to sprinkle themselves with its water and pray for children, was based on belief in the generative, life-giving powers of water. Girls who were going to be married were called nymphs, a word that means "veiled" (with the bridal veil). As lesser divinities (demi-gods), nymphs at first had no temples dedicated to them, but only sacred sites and altars, and they were worshipped in woods and caves, at fountains and springs, that is, in all those places where their presence was felt. Later, small temples or "nymphaea" were dedicated to them; these elegant buildings were built both in cities and in the country and were the venue for marriage ceremonies.

However, for the practical-minded Romans the concept of nymphs was quite another thing, since they were not so accustomed to interpreting the spirit of their cult, which they imported without spiritual participation. As a result, the nymphaea-temples were gradually replaced by nymphaea used as pleasure gardens, places for physical and spiritual relief located in large complexes that included villas and houses. Having no sentimental or symbolic associations, the Roman nymphaeum became popular for its purely ornamental aspects, enhanced as it was by fountains and elaborate decoration that suggested the idea of a cave, an immersion in Nature artificially created Nature that, despite its masterly conception, had lost its emotional and spiritual vitality. The cool, well-organized Roman nymphaeum was far removed from the bewitching seductiveness of the nymphs. However, near fountains and springs, there are a few nymphaea that have retained the ancient enchantment of the cult, where one can still find the original spirit, the *locus nymphae*, with its prophetic and vital attributes.

Opposite: detail of the fresco decoration in the Auditorium of Maecenas.

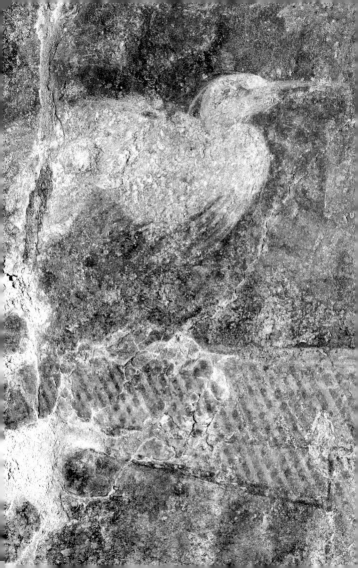

14 – The Nymphaeum of Egeria

What better imaginable setting is there for Numa Pompilio's trysts with the beautiful nymph Egeria than the grotto named after her? We can see them meeting, amid the sound of flowing water, in the shade of wisteria and creeping plants.

It must be said that this is truly one of the few cases in which myth gives life to the site and the site in turn gives shape to the myth. The grotto of Egeria–so hard to reach in the vast Caffarella park that is seems to have been hidden on purpose in order to be appreciated only by the judicious– embodies the nymph's prophetic secrets, leaving an indelible impression on those who discover it after a long walk through lanes, footpaths and woods. Livy offers a description: "There was once a wood, the middle of which was irrigated by a perennial spring that gushed out of a shady grotto. And since Numa very often went there alone, as if he were to meet with the goddess, he consecrated that wood to the Camenae, since it was here that they met with Egeria, his consort."

The grotto, visited by such famous travellers as Stendhal and Goethe, has retained its Arcadian spirit. The entrance is barely visible among the thick vegetation in the Caffarella park. It is only natural for us to think back on the time when the Corybantes, the priestesses of the Phrygian goddess Cybele, ran through these cool clearings, screaming wildly to the frenetic beating of drums and the clashing of cymbals. When spring arrived, the devotees of Cybele would go from the sacrarium on the top of the Palatine Hill to the point where the Almone river flows into the Tiber to perform the sacred *lavatio Matris Deum* rite. As Ovid relates, "There is a place where the rapid Almone flows into the Tiber / and loses its name in that greater river. / The white-haired priest with vermilion garments / there with that water washes the goddess and the sacred objects. / The procession shouts, the tibia resounds wildly, / the hands of the eunuchs beat on the drums." It is almost as if we can see the castrated priests of the goddess, the Great Mother of the Gods, engrossed in washing the sacred instruments and the black stone,

Opposite: the nymphaeum in the Caffarella park.

meteorite from Pessinus, which the ancients considered her effigy and symbolic simulacrum. The spell is broken and that valley returns to its present state of abandon: the salubrious, clear waters of the Almone are now an embanked ditch, an unbecoming sewer frequented by rats. And yet in ancient times the valley with its woods and brooks flowing into bodies of water was an enchanting place with an idyllic and sacred atmosphere–a *locus amoeni* or garden of delights, the perfect spot to build one's country home. This is exactly what Herodes Atticus (101- 179 A.D.) did as soon as he acquired that vast property, between the 2nd and 3rd milestones of the Appian Way and the Asinaria, from his wife. An able politician, philosopher, rhetorician and patron of the arts, he had this luxurious residence built in honour of his young wife, Annia Regilla, using the land she had brought to him with her dowry.

It was an enormous villa decorated with porticoes, temples and sacred precincts. Its singular name, Triopion, may have derived from the Thessalian hero Triopas, who violated the temple of Demeter. The com-

An 18th-century engraving of the interior of the Nymphaeum of Egeria in Herodes Atticus' Triopion.

plex was both rural and celebratory, and was sacred to the Manes and all Annia Regilla's tutelary gods of the underworld.

Of the few remains of what was a sumptuous complex, mention should be made of the so-called nymphaeum of Egeria, a building erected in the 2nd century A.D. as one of the villa's amenities. Once inside the damp grotto with water dripping from the top and walls, it is hard to imagine what it must have looked like; and it is also difficult to recall that it is man-made, because it blended in so well with its natural setting. Its walls dotted with niches were once dressed with green marble, but are now covered with mildew, and water runs off them into the canals below. Nothing remains of the walls that once glittered with marble, the serpentine pavements, the niches with shells and coloured mosaics, the statues and porticoes. Nature has taken this site back into her fold, covering it with mildew and lichens, sparing only the tender, vibrating shadow of the "goddess nymph dear to the Muses, who was the wife of Numa and his councilor" (Ovid).

A sculpture piece in the nymphaeum.

15 – The Nymphaeum of the Annibaldi

Lost in the bright marble facing of the wall on Via degli Annibaldi is a small iron gate whose modest appearance is misleading, since it conceals a lovely relic of antiquity consisting of small waterfalls and watercourses. Once part of a sumptuous villa, it reveals a world made up of exquisite stuccowork, smooth multicoloured plaster, glass, ornamental fountains, murmuring canals, and whatever else would give pleasure to its sophisticated owners at the threshold of the Imperial Age.

A spiral staircase goes down into the depths of the hill, like leading us on a journey into the *interior terrae*. We forget the present as we penetrate the crevice, proceeding into that rarified remnant from the past, and come upon a small nymphaeum.

While descending, an arabesque of alternating shields and light pilaster strips appears before us. A crusty carpet of stuccoes and shells constituting lozenges, shields and cuirasses marks the way to the nyphaeum niches, until we begin to make out an apse, which was truncated in modern times. The four niches, which must orginally have been nine in number, introduce us to a vast hall, at the end of which is a pool. The flashes of light created by the statues and sculptures once alternated with the brown and earth hues of the pumice and stuccowork in an elegant harmony of colours animated by the reflections of the water. The delicate relief decoration and the reticulate masonry walls, made up of small blocks of tufa, remind us of the splendour of the late Republican Age.

But once inside, historic dates and facts, construction periods and building styles, have little meaning. As if engulfed in the flux of Time, we find ourselves at the very origin of myth, and the archetypal nymphaeum, the site sacred to nymphs, reveals their way of interpreting the intimate essence of water. Thus, the spirit of place brings this site back to life.

Opposite: detail of the apse in the nymphaeum.

16 – The Auditorium of Maecenas

Beneath a sloping roof behind the rough surface of its outer walls, the Auditorium of Maecenas conceals the nobility of its past from the bleak buildings around it. It seems to be offering shelter to those who wish to escape from the chaos of modern life and rediscover here an Arcadian atmosphere made up of gardens and pleasure-grounds for erudite, literary conversation. And this monument also seems to tell us that before Caius Maecenas transformed the area into the *Horti Mecenatiani*, the scenery must have been completely different.

The hill, the domain of prostitutes and stray dogs, corpses and sorcerers, was an unhealthy, miserable sight indeed. But after Maecenas' work it regained its original pride and dignity. "Nowadays people can live on the reclaimed Esquiline," writes Horace, "and stroll in the sun on the ramparts, from which one had a view of the desolate land become white with bleached bones. As for me, I am not so troubled by the thieves and animals that once infested this spot, as by the witches who with potions and magic spells try to upset the human mind."

The villa was surrounded by gardens consisting of an infinite variety of plants, statues and various buildings, of which only the auditorium remains. A sloping ramp descends to the long, straight hall with an apse at its end. It is easy to reconstruct the scene in our mind, with the dinner guests lying on couches while they watched the spectacle of the rushing water. The sound of citharas and flutes mingled with that of the water, and the cascade fell rhythmically over the variegated colour of the cipolin steps, flowing into the long canal in the middle of the hall. Sheltered from the sultry summer heat, Maecenas' illustrious banquet guests refreshed their bodies and minds with odes and songs. Then the symposium became noisy and somewhat rowdy, so much so that we can almost visualize that merry company described by Horace, "who do not refuse a glass of old Massic wine and spend part of the day lying in the shade of a strawberry tree or by the spring where the water of a nymph murmurs sweetly."

Opposite: the back wall of the vestibule has most of the epigraphs found during the digs.

In that scene with its artificial verdure, the stepped tiers, decorated with plants and flowers, lend a certain pleasant naturalness to the place. Light blue and Pompeiian red are the coloured backdrop to the plants, birds and fruit painted with swift, delicate brushstrokes. The frescoed decoration of abundant nature covers those walls. It does not matter if the birds' chirping is false and the shrubs in front of illusory windows are the result of masterfully wrought artifice; after all, art is the queen of deception. But our amazement does not end here, as the brown frieze draws our gaze away from the sweet enchantment of those gardens and focusses on the swarm of evanescent little figures dashing about against a black background. Fleshy satyrs and maenads crop up from the eroded plaster, as we catch a glimpse of their faces and features, clothes and movements. A she-goat stubbornly resisting Pan's invitation to be sacrificed is followed by a Silenus on a donkey,

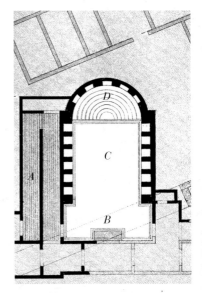

while further on is a frenetic dance of Bacchantes. This is a Bacchic procession moving to the sound of a double flute. Perhaps some form of initiation, participation in the Dionysian mysteries, was necessary to give "meaning" to these images. Thus, penetrating the secrets of their world, of their regeneration through nature, its birth and rebirth, its inner mystery, we would discover the supreme values of that symposium. By entering that hall everything would become clear, even the epigram by Callimachus on the outer wall of the semi-circular end of the hall: "Should I come to thee drunk on purpose, reproach me, oh Archinus; but if I did so without wanting to, then excuse my audacity. Wine and Love held me in their grip; the one drove me on and the other held me back from giving vent to that audacity. And when I came I did not understand who he is and whose son he is, but I kissed the threshold. And if this be a fault, then I am guilty."

Opposite: plan of the nymphaeum (A, entrance; B, vestibule; C, summer triclinium; D, apse).
Above: general view of the hall.

Sacred Sites

In this context, the word "sacred" applies to both pagan and Christian buildings used for religious purposes. This definition may be debatable, but it is useful in dealing with temples, parish churches and sanctuaries from the specific vantage point of religion in Roman culture. From the conventional pagan areas with their temples to the Middle Eastern sanctuaries and the Christian titles (parish churches in Rome whose titular head is a cardinal), we can follow a path that goes from the more traditional forms of worship in the pagan pantheon to the more complex circumstances of the "crisis" in Middle Eastern religion, down to Christianity. This is a path that, despite the limited number of examples given, clearly exemplifies the various stages in the evolution of, and historical continuity toward, monotheistic religion, with all the architectural and formal relevance this implies.

Opposite: detail of the mosaic in the Via Livenza hypogeum.
Above: decorative element in the S. Martino ai Monti complex.

17 – The Largo Argentina Sacred Precinct

At the end of the Pigna quarter, a group of small medieval houses, patrician mansions and churches once concealed a more ancient site. This was discovered by chance during the construction of a large building in 1918 that was never finished. What remained was a small sunken square surrounded by trees and containing a forest of columns. Because of its location, the ancient site was called the Largo Argentina sacred precinct.

The enclosure has four temples, one behind the other, with several altars standing in front of them, which cannot but make us think of the time when the precinct was a religious site of primary importance. Since the divinities to which they were dedicated have not been determined with certainty and only interesting but unproved hypotheses have been formulated, the temples are known as A, B, C and D.

The most ancient one is C, the third in line from the Largo Argentina, dating from the late 4th century-early 3rd century B.C. Standing on a tufa podium, it has preserved its archaic *sine postico* configuration (that is, the temple is closed by the rear wall of the cella). Some scholars think the temple may have been dedicated to Feronia, an ancient Italic goddess who uttered her prophecies at the foot of Mt. Soracte. The second temple in chronological order is A (the first from the right), the cella of which supports the apses of the small medieval church of S. Nicola de' Calcario. A peripteral hexastyle edifice, it was most probably dedicated to Juturna and was built in 241 B.C. by Caius Lutatius Catulus after the naval victory against the Carthaginians near the Aegadian Islands. The last temple in the row, and the third oldest, is D, which is made entirely of travertine and considered the centre of the cult of the *Lares permarini*, the protectors of the seaways.

Lastly is Temple B, the largest and most beautiful, a round structure with a ring of columns that breaks the rigid axial rhythm of the other three temples. It contains the remains of a colossal acrolith with

Opposite: view of the round Temple B, with its remaining columns.

female features that some scholars suggest is *Fortuna Huiusce Diei* (Good Fortune Today). The temple was founded by Quintus Lutatius Catulus, who was consul in 101 B.C. with Marius after the victory over the Cimbri at Vercelli.

The Largo Argentina is a large archaeological precinct with major Republican Age temples that were initially disassociated, a religious site that has been changed quite a lot over the centuries but has preserved its sacred character. The temples all underwent rebuilding and restoration that altered their structure, which in any case had originally passed through various building stages. In fact, their interiors contain hidden altars, podia, pavements and favissae, and under the modest tufa dressing is a labyrinth of underground passageways that open onto unexpected crevices in the very heart of the temple. This interesting architectural maze of ruins bears witness to changes and vicissitudes on the site such as fires and social and religious developments—a precious testimony of history.

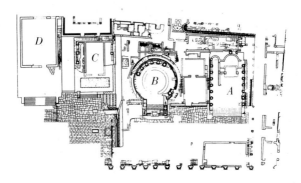

Above: plan of the sacred precinct with the aligned temples.
Opposite: an underground gallery under Temple A.

18 – Three Temples in the Forum Holitorium

Vegetables were a staple in the ancient Romans' diet, especially among the lower classes. Almost all Romans had a small kitchen garden which provided them with most of their food. When this did not suffice they would go to the fruit and vegetable market, the *Forum Holitorium*, which was situated near the port on the Tiber, in the area between the Capitoline Hill, the Theatre of Marcellus and the Tiber, outside the Servian city walls. The commercial importance of this area was substantiated by the public granaries and the Forum Boarium, which had a bronze bull from Aegina to indicate its function as a cattle market. The Forum Holitorium, on the other hand, had a marble elephant called *Elephas herbarius*.

As early as the end of the Republican Age the Forum Holitorium had been transformed into a monumental square, acquiring temples and porticoes; and when the Theatre of Marcellus was inaugurated in 11 B.C., the forum was beautified with a travertine pavement. Three temples with aligned façades occupied the west side of the forum. The first of these was Doric, rather small and peripteral (surrounded by columns). The second, middle one was also a peripteral hexastyle structure, but was Ionic, while the third, again with a six-column façade, was of the Italic Ionic type–that is, it had colonnades on three sides and was closed in the rear by a wall (peripteral *sine postico*).

Assigning names to these temples is not easy, but historical sources indicate they may be the temples of Spes (Hope), Juno Sospita (the Saviour), and Janus. The same sources mention another temple, known as Pietas, which was built by Manlius Acilius Glabro during the battle of Thermopylae. This temple was short-lived (191-189 B.C.), as it was demolished to make room for the Theatre of Marcellus. A legend grew up around this temple that helps to explain the place name "in Carcere" (in prison) added to the church of S. Nicola, which incorporated the lower parts of those temples. Pliny relates the story as follows: "A maiden of the lower class, hence unknown, had a mother who

Opposite: view of the ruins of the temples.

was being kept in prison as punishment. Having asked to go inside, but being driven out by the custodian for fear she would bring food to her mother, the girl was caught by surprise one day while suckling her mother with her breasts. After this miracle the mother was let free and consecrated to the goddess Pietas, together with the place itself, and both women were granted nourishment for the rest of their lives. This occurred during the consulate of C. Quinctius and M. Acilius; therefore, on the site of the prison the temple of Pietas was constructed, where the Theatre of Marcellus now stands." The legend originated in Greece and continued to be known throughout the Middle Ages, the figure of the father replacing that of the mother. In fact it was so widespread that it inspired writers and painters: from Caravaggio to Byron, the tale was the basis for the theme of charity and compassion. The crypt under the high altar in the church of S. Nicola in Carcere leads to the subterranean section. This church's foundation stands on the central temple of Juna Sospita, the side aisles extending into the spaces between the three temples, so that the side walls of the church incorporate the outer colonnades of the two side temples. Beneath the

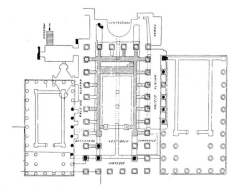

Above: plan of the sacred precinct with the three temples.
Opposite: Jean Barbault, Ruins of the Holitorium *(watercolour).*

left-hand aisle of the church is a long corridor that allows one to catch a glimpse, to the right, of the tall plinths of the six Doric columns of the temple supposedly dedicated to Spes, and, to the right, the foundations of the central temple.

This passageway is suspended between the two edifices and reveals all the virtues of temple architecture, with its harmonious sequence of spaces and columns and the alignment of the podia. Halfway past the left-hand wall is a three-section cella which, because of its particular shape, was probably constructed at a later date, perhaps in the Byzantine age. Under the church nave the long hall has the remains of the foundations of the central temple, and its innermost part contains the favissae (storehouses for ex-voto offerings). The third passageway reveals the entire side of the Italic-style Ionic temple, with the plinths of the seven columns wedged into the right-hand wall of the basilica. The sight of the temple's stylobates, with the plinths and lower shafts of the columns, in no way detracts from the evident traces of commercial life that took place around these three temples: small shops that sold drinks, sweets or religious souvenirs.

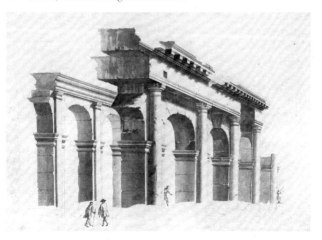

19 – The Syriac Sanctuary on the Janiculum

Near a spring on the slopes of the Janiculum hill are the remains of a Syriac sanctuary. Here, in the woods, there grew up a cult that had originated in the Middle East and worshipped the demoniacal, vindictive Italic diety Furrina. This is a grim site, marked by its terrible *genius loci* and disturbing crimes. The sanctuary was discovered in 1906, when an excavation campaign brought to light three different building phases, only the last of which is easy to interpret.

On the other bank of the Tiber, far from the official cults and institutional liturgies, the foreign communities of slaves, freedmen and nouveaux riches had their own rituals and idols, and the complexities of their mystery cults were therefore assimilated into the traditional

pantheon. For example, the *Regio XIV* (fourth district) embraced the transcendental aspirations of the Middle East, with their emphasis on redemption and their concepts of death and resurrection.

The first temple that was constructed on this site, in the form of a *tèmenos* with a basin or sacred pool, is to be considered in this context, as is its subsequent transformation on the part of a certain Gaionas, a rich and generous Syrian who had brought his religious beliefs and rituals to Rome. The earliest sanctuary was destroyed for unknown reasons and was rebuilt in the 4th century A.D. in a different style and with a different orientation. This is the edifice we see today. It must have been totally enclosed, with three distinct wings: in

View from the courtyard of the hall with a basilica plan.

the middle was a courtyard, to the west was a building with a basilica plan, and, to the east, lay another octagonal structure. Curiously enough, the orientation of the temple was corrected by eight degrees between the outside walls and the short inner ones, so that the temple axis would be perfectly aligned toward the east, that is, in the direction of the rising sun, in keeping with religious tradition.

The courtyard separated the two main edifices. The one with a basilica plan was used for public liturgies, while the octagonal one was reserved for mystery rituals. The former has three sections–the middle nave, wider than the two side aisles, all three with niches–which has led scholars to think that three divinities were worshipped here. And since a headless statue seated on a throne found in the central apse can be interpreted, in the Syriac context, as Jupiter Heliopolitanus (*Hadad*, or Jupiter Serapis), it may be that the other two deities were those that completed the Heliopolitan trinity: Atargatis (the ancient Roman goddess Syria) and her son Simios (Mercury for the Romans, later associated with Dionysus). A strange foundation ritual must have had something to do with the establishment of the cult, since under the level of Jupiter-Hadad's niche archaeologists found a skull without its teeth and lower jaw that disappeared under mysterious circumstances after being discovered.

But this is not the only mystery. In the multiform section of the temple facing east, archaeologists discovered a black basalt Egyptian statue (from the apse) and another statue of Dionysus with gilded hands and face. Another small bronze idol was found lying on its back inside a triangular altar: a young embalmed man wrapped in the seven coils of a snake that rests its head on that of the youth. Together with this discovery, archaeologists found seven eggs arranged in a symbolic manner. Naturally, this amazing find triggered a passionate search for the identity and role of this singular idol, which are by no means clear. It is certainly a deity with Egyptian-Syrian attributes, a syncretized sun god who dies and is reborn. Whether it is Simios or Adonis, or, more probably, Osiris or Dionysus, the only certainty we have is that it represents a mystery cult associated with redemption.

Opposite: the bronze statuette found inside a triangular altar.

20 – S. Crisogono

The *Regio XIV*, present-day Trastevere, was a district on the right-hand bank of the Tiber with a mixed poulation, mostly Jews and Syrians, of the middle and lower classes engaged in commercial activities. This was a social context quite receptive to the new Christian eucumenism. Trastevere bears witness to its Early Christian past in the names of its ancient basilicas, the *tituli* or titles. When in 1907, while exploring the area under the sacristy of S. Chrisogono church, the Trinitarian fathers L. Manfredini and C. Piccolini discovered a semi-circular wall, they had no idea that they had chanced upon one of the most interesting examples of an Early Christian basilica. Subsequent research brought to light, about six metres under the level of the present-day basilica, the remains of the earliest church and the late Imperial Age structure on which it had been built.

As the excavation progressed, archaeologists unearthed a fine pave-ment of inlaid marble, the presbytery area and a *schola cantorum*, which helped researchers to mark out the confines of a religious building with an aisleless nave (a rarity in Rome), a portico and an apse. This is an unusual structure, not only because of the nave, but also for the presence of two structures on either side of the apse of clearly Eastern origin. These were called *pastophoria* and were

Below: detail of the frescoes found along the north wall.

Opposite: the left side of the titulus *apse with the crypt and relics chamber.*

used as service rooms. The one on the right must have been the *dia-conicum*, a sort of sacristy. The other was probably the *protesis*, a storeroom for the sacred objects; however, the fact that basins were found there would seem to indicate that this was not its function. In fact, the excavation journal speaks of a basin "with an unusual shape [the basin that is still visible], carved out of the south wall, and other large rectangular basins that form a network of communicating water recipients [that no longer exist], with drainage channels leading to a broad covered sewer." These earlier structures have led some scholars to believe the chamber was once a *fullonica*, a laundry and dye-house, while others claim that the basin carved out of one wall was used for immersion baptism. When the basilica was built, the chamber on the left became more monumental in appearance with the addition of doors and windows. The rectangular basins were covered and marble dressing was put on the middle one, perhaps with the aim of making the hall into a baptistery. So it was there that the faithful, in the ritual of Christian initiation, were baptized by immersion.

The *domus* was named after Chrysogonus, the founder of the original church (*conditor tituli*), who it seems was neither a martyr nor a saint, but simply one of the devout and rich patrons who offered their homes to the first Christian communities in the district. Despite this, the *titulus Chrysogoni* soon became the *titulus Sancti Chrysogoni*, thus conferring an aura of sanctity to the owner.

A stairway leads down to the subterranean, horseshoe-shaped ambulatory that ran under the apse to form the crypt. The straight part of this crypt was decorated with paintings, of which only three hieratic figures of saints remain. They were executed when Pope Gregory III (731-741) decided to make drastic changes to the basilica: he raised the presbytery by about 1.60 metres, restored its roof and had its walls decorated with frescoes. We can still see the painted section on the top part of the apse wall, which has disks inside lozenges and other curious geometric motifs. The cella for

Opposite, above: plan of the basilica plan complex.
Opposite, below: a part of the apse wall.

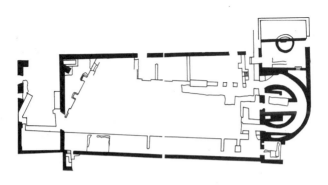

the holy relics, the focal point of religious devotion, was built in the crypt. Here, by means of two *fenestellae confessionis*, the faithful hoped to acquire some of the sanctity of the relics by putting their white clothing on sticks and pushing them through these small windows to touch the relics or get close to them.

Proceeding along the passageway, one sees some sarcophagi, which show that some parts of the basilica were used as a burial site. The nave gives one the impression of having two side aisles, since the space is divided into three sections by the foundation walls of the upper church. The rough walls bear traces of frescoes here and there. On the right-hand wall are the remains of a fresco cycle depicting the life of St. Benedict, painted on two registers and bordered at the bottom by the usual drapery motif. Consequently we can assume that the rest of the basilica was decorated with frescoes, in keeping with the policy of richly decorating the Early Christian churches in Rome.

Above: sarcophagus marble relief depicting a procession of sea creatures.
Opposite: detail of the frescoes found on the north wall.

21 – S. Cecilia in Trastevere

This church, with its many superposed layers of building material, can be considered a perfect example of how different periods have left their traces over the centuries. The oldest stratum, which was found in 1899, has a Republican Age dwelling that was enlarged and then rebuilt, incorporating another house built in the same period. These alterations, which took place from the time of the Republic to the 4th century A.D., transformed the original nature of the structure so much that scholars suggested the complex–lacking the typical features of a Roman *domus*–was to be viewed as part of the commercial and artisan area on the other side of the Tiber river. The presence in one of the buildings of eight brick basins seemed to confirm this theory. Two pre-Constantinian registers–the *Curiosum* and the *Description of the Regions*–led these scholars to think it was a tannery. The proximity of the river and the enlargement of the new port of the emporium had given rise to the creation of a settlement populated by artisans, small tradesmen, millers (there were several mills on the river), labourers and immigrants from Middle Eastern countries (the Jewish community was the largest).

However, research carried out to date has not furnished enough data to allow archaeologists to identify any of these places as the house traditionally considered the site of St. Cecilia's martyrdom. The fact that there is a heating system (hypocaust) in the so-called *balneum Cæciliae* is not sufficient to back up the tradition, especially in view of the fact that the account of the saint's martyrdom dates from the late 5th century A.D. and therefore cannot be considered a reliable historical source. Nevertheless, there is no doubt that those rooms, which were made part of the same complex around the 4th century A.D., were inhabited by a Christian community, or better, by a church named after its founder.

A recent study has revealed a continuous relationship between the saint and the archaic *Bona Dea* pagan cult, which was centered

Opposite: the hall leading to the subterranean rooms, now a small antiquarium.

near the basilica. This pagan divinity–whose nature was rather mysterious and confusing, especially in the rituals carried out in her name–was linked to the charitable healing of the ill. In fact, her main attribute was that of *Oclatra, resiturix luminum*, a restorer of sight, and this is directly connected to the name of the saint (Cæcilia and *cæcitas*, or blindness). Furthermore, some prayers recited in ancient times in the Trastevere basilica (which have words such as *resitutor*) is further evidence of a sort of appropriation of the pagan divinity's attributes on the part of the Christian saint.

The sacristy leads to the underground section, which has a large area that has been interpreted as being the peristyle of the *domus Cæciliae*. The epigraphs, sculptures, plutei and fragments all over the walls help to create the gloomy and ancient atmosphere of an antiquarium. A maze of rooms and corridors connected by walls,

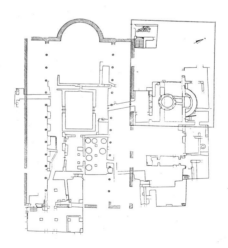

Above: plan of the archaeological precinct, with the basilica.
Opposite: the room in front of the lararium, with amphorae on display.

piers and areas of patchwork is indicative of a laborious and complex building process. The pavements are on several strata and have different elements and styles, thus adding to the complexity of the architecture: one passes from rich, multicoloured patterns to ordinary *opus spicatum* (herringbone) pavements and then to elegant tesselated work. A sort of corridor leads to a rectangular room to the right that is enclosed by a solid brick wall; the seven round brick basins in the pavement are clear signs that this was a tannery.

Proceeding through the ambulatory, we go down into a large hall with finely wrought fluted sarcophagi and other interesting objects. This room in turn affords access to another one, which is one of the most ancient in this underground site, as can been seen by the wall at the end made of blocks of tufa and the Doric column opposite. On the floor is a heap of amphoras and vases, and in the room opposite

is a *lararium* or shrine inside a small niche, which transform what was an austere and is gloomy setting into the warm and hospitable intimacy of an ancient Roman *domus*. The archaic image of the goddess Minerva, made of simple clay, is seen in profile with her helmet and sceptre and is accompanied by a maenad and a sacrifice scene. Further along the corridor, a narrow passageway at left has two tufa columns; they date from the earliest building period of the site and mark the end of this side of the structure. Proceeding down the corridor, you come upon an area of singular richness and colour–a Neo-Byzantine crypt that was laid out in the late 19th-early 20th century, consisting of a host of small columns supporting *velaria* ornated with stuccowork and studded with mosaics. This lively, eclectic composition helps to attenuate the gloominess of the subterranean setting, providing, if only for a moment, an ornamental interlude to this austere ancient site.

Above: the niche with the shrine.
Opposite: a corridor lined with epigraphs.

124

22 – S. Clemente

With its many superposed layers of architecture and history, the church of S. Clemente is one of the best examples of the growth of the Eternal City. A monumental staircase flanked by archaeological finds and stone epigraphs leads down to the subterranean areas. The first stop is what must have been the narthex of the lower basilica, or better, the ancient *titulus Clementis*.

St. Clement was the object of great veneration as well as the subject of a host of legends handed down to us in the *Letteratura Clementina* and the 4th-century *Acta*. These apocryphal sources tell us that the saint, who was sent into exile in the Crimea during Trajan's rule, embarked on proselytizing activity and was punished for this by being tied to an anchor and thrown into the sea. Some time later the water receded, revealing an islet with the splendid tomb of St. Clement built by angels. Since that time, the tide went out every year, revealing the tomb.

This miracle is illustrated on the walls of the narthex by an unknown late 11th-century painter, who drew inspiration for the two painted panels from the story narrated in the *Acta*. From the episode of the child carried away by the waves after visiting the tomb and then miraculously found, to the translation of the saint's body, St. Clement's life is skilfully narrated in detail. There is also a dedica-

Above: the sacrophagus found in the lower church.
Opposite: the walls along the nave facing the narthex of the lower church.

tion, as well as the portrait of the donors in the lower part of the fresco: a certain Benone de Rapiz and his wife Maria Macellari and their children, Clemente and Altilia, who are depicted commending themselves to the mercy of God with their gift.

The narthex affords glimpses into the nave. The left-hand corner is the one with the most frescoes, a sort of resumé of the wide range of 11th-century Roman painting, which departed from the formalism of Byzantine art and created a more popular idiom. The left-hand section has scenes from the New Testament: an Ascension (or perhaps an Assumption), with a space set aside for the relic; the Crucifixion; the Holy Women at Christ's Tomb; the Marriage at Cana; the Descent into Limbo. All these frescoes date from the 9th century, but do not stir our admiration as much as the 11th-century ones nearby representing scenes from the life of St. Alexis.

Above: detail of the low-relief on the sarcophagus depicting the myth of Hippolytus.
Opposite: detail of the nave fresco representing the Mass of St. Clement.

When he was a young man, this saint from Rome ran away from home on his wedding day and spent years going on pilgrimages and living the life of a hermit. Upon his return, his father, Senator Euphemianus, did not recognize him and hired him as a servant, and his son lived for 17 years below the stairs of his own house. When he was about to die, Alexis sent a letter to the Pope in which he described his life, and the Pope in turn narrated the story to the saint's father and his abandoned bride. His story, depicted so vividly in the frescoes of the ancient lower church, certainly impressed the faithful deeply.

Next to these paintings is the legend of Sisinnius, the prefect of Rome who tried to capture St. Clement while he was saying mass but was suddenly struck blind. In the register below these frescoes are Sisinnius' servants, who have also become blind, struggling to

drag a column that they have mistaken for the Pope. This episode is famous for the servants' surprisingly coarse language: "Fili de la pute, traite, Gosmari, Albertel, traite. Falite derto colo palo, Carvoncelle!" (Pull, you sons of bitches, pull Gosmari and Albertel. And you, Carvoncello, use some elbow grease with the pole!). Such vulgar language is commented on laconically in Latin by St. Clement in the upper register: "Duritiam cordis vesti. Saxa trahere meruisti" (With your hard hearts you deserve to drag stones). "Tit for tat" between the vernacular Italian and the official Latin, between the lofty scenes of the saint's life and the more common ones below them, exemplify the artist's innovative spirit and his efforts to render the hagiographic episodes in a more descriptive manner.

Another noteworthy sight is the double apse, Roman and medieval, that rounds off the nave. One can walk in the blind area from here. In the right-hand aisle, in an 8th-9th century niche, is an austere enthroned Madonna surrounded by Byzantine saints wearing diadems. But even more fascinating is the large 1st-century A.D. sarcophagus on which are sculpted scenes of the story of Phaedra and Hippolytus. In the left-hand aisle, besides the modern altar of saints Cyril and Metodius, is a round structure that may have been an ancient font for baptism by immersion, but may also have been a fountain or even a wine-press.

The right-hand aisle affords access to the level below (the third) by means of a steep stairway that leads into a maze of 1st-century A.D. rooms that are connected to one another. Here, with the aid of some floorplans, it is possible to find the building on which the Christian *titulus* or title church was founded. Situated beyond the passage that divides the rooms on this level, is a large rectangular structure built with large tufa blocks that support the brick walls resting on travertine. On the other side of this passage is a less imposing building, which was perhaps an *insula*, divided into small apartments laid out around a courtyard on which the Mithraic temple was built in a later period.

A Byzantine-style Madonna and Child (8th-9th century).

23 – S. Martino ai Monti

Watched over by the Capocci towers, the basilica of S. Martino ai Monti rises up with its apse on top of the Esquiline Hill, its foundation resting on the massive blocks of tufa of the ancient Servian Walls. This church, with its singular arrangement, is typical of the historical and architectural continuity in Rome from the Imperial Age to the present.

The various levels–the most ancient of which dates back to the 3rd century A.D.–is of great interest for the history of early Christianity, because this was probably the site of the original *titulus Equitii*, the first titular church of Equitius.

This church lies under S. Martino ai Monti and can be reached via the crypt of the latter. It is still not known whether it was founded over a more ancient building (a covered market, according to some scholars) or whether it was built in the 3rd century to meet the needs of the cult. The earliest information we have comes from the *Liber Pontificalis*, which tells us that it is a Constantinian age titular church linked to the name of Pope Sylvester, whose famous deeds are illustrated in the lively frescoes in the Santi Quattro Coronati Church oratory. The last documentation dates from the

Above: fragment of the frescoes of the original medieval decoration.
Opposite: the underground chambers entrance hall and the vestibule.

8th century, after which time all memory of the original titular church vanished. Only during restoration work carried out in the 17th century was this buried church brought to light by the prior of the San Martino monastery. This discovery caused such a stir that Cardinal Barberini decided to have copies made of all the frescoes for a codex that is still in the Vatican Library (Cod. Barb. Lat. 4405).

The underground area is an irregular rectangle oriented almost precisely East-West. Two rows of thick piers divide the hall into eleven bays that have at least three different types of masonry corresponding to three building periods. Originally this hall was most probably a large rectangular space with a mosaic pavement of black and white tesserae in a checkerboard pattern (this can still be seen in some parts of the hall). The whole room was plastered and frescoed, and had an adjoining courtyard which is partly visible to the northwest. The complex also contained two upper floors that were demolished in a later period. It may have been a block of flats, an *insula* with luxury apartments, or a covered market. At a certain stage the edifice was subject to a drastic change, becoming a Christian place of worship. Fragments of frescoes depicting scenes from the life of Christ decorated the rooms and all the walls were dressed with marble.

The religious function of the building was maintained even after the construction of the upper basilica and monastery (9th century), which is proof of the importance attached to its religious legacy.

Above: part of the polychrome decoration on a wall.
Opposite: the tomb cover found during the digs.

IO: BAPTISTAE RVBEO RAVENNAT
GEN: MEL: F. ORDINIS GENERALI
QVI: MORIBVS: ET: DOCTRINA
CLARVS: VIXO: QVI: ORDINEM: VA
ANNOS: XVI: REXIT: AC: PRIVILEGIIS
A: GREGORIO: XIII: PONT: MAX: IMPETRATIS
ILLVSTRAVIT: VIXIT: ANNOS: LXXI: OBIIT:
ANNO: M: D: LXXVII: DECESSIT: NONIS:
SEPTEMBRIS

24 – SS. Giovanni e Paolo

The slopes of the Caelian Hill bear traces of a strong ongoing relationship with the past. Under the arches of the *Clivus Scauri* street we find ourselves in another age, or better, in other ages. The SS. Giovanni e Paolo Basilica is another link with the past, honouring the memory of the original titular church attributed to a certain Pammachius, *vir eruditis et nobilis*, who died in 410 A.D. Behind its Baroque lavishness, the church seems to be concealing its ancient past, and once we have crossed the threshold of a nondescript door we will discover all its history. The bright nave contrasts with a crowded, dark maze of rooms arranged on different levels that extends into the subterranean recesses of the basilica.

This complex of rooms includes an *insula* or multi-storey apartment house that at the beginning of the 3rd century A.D. incorporated other buildings dating from the 2nd century. Afterwards the complex was taken over by a single owner, at a time when there were clear signs of a conversion to Christianity. The frescoes with pagan subjects were covered and between the two *domus* a small room, probably a *confessio*, was frescoed with stories of martyrs.

The intricate complex of rooms built one after the other can be said to have three building phases: the Roman pagan house, the pagan-Christian one, and the early medieval oratory. The first room we see has basins, which indicate it was a nymphaeum. There is a fresco on the back wall with a large coloured background representing a legend difficult to identify; it may be Proserpine's return from Hades or, more probably, a cycle on Venus, with the goddess of love in company with Peitho and Bacchus. Two female figures, one fully dressed and the other nude but covered with jewels, seem to be receiving an homage or greeting from a standing male figure who is turning toward them with a goblet in one hand and a bunch of grapes in the other. The scene is set against a background depicting the sea populated with putti fishing and playing in their boats.

Opposite: a corridor leading to the chamber containing the holy relics.

This vividly rendered blaze of light blue and ochre with splashes of vermilion is one of the highest achievements of Roman painting in the period from the late 2nd century and the early 3rd century A.D. Equally interesting is the decoration of the adjacent triclinium: the vault is animated by putti climbing up grapevines and harvesting grapes, supported by a train of genii with well-proportioned nude bodies holding cloaks behind them. Peacocks, thrushes and roosters are a delightful addition, either soaring in the air or dancing on the ground in a rhythmical pattern marked out by the genii.

The next room, which archaeologists think is a *tablinum*, has walls decorated simply with imitation marble panels, but the vault has a composition with an obvious Christian subject. Apostles and animals face one another in sections of a circle as if they were revolving on a catherine wheel. The figures with togas and scrolls, either prophets or apostles, closely correspond to Christian iconographic tradition and, presumedly, so does the representation of the *mulctra*, the milk bucket between two sheep which symbolizes both comfort and life-blood. But there is no doubt about the Early Christian roots of the

representation of the orant dressed in an elegant dalmatic, his arms outspread, emulating Christ's sacrifice (4th century A.D.).

Next is the *confessio* recess, with the tomb of the martyrs that the faithful can see through the *fenestella confessionis*. Here, with the fresco narrating the martyrdom of Sts. Crispus, Crispinian and Benedicta, who were imprisoned by Roman soldiers and then beheaded, we sense we are in the very heart of the ancient liturgical tradition. The drama of martyrdom is followed by that of heavenly redemption; the back wall, with the fresco of Sts. John and Paul and the Redeemer in an orant's attitude being worshipped by the faithful, is a promise of paradise.

Going back to a small stairway that leads to the baths below, everything seems gloomy and oppressive in the darkness. Here it is not easy to sense the delights this site once provided with its mosaic pavement, purificatory basins and hot steam baths.

The fresco on the back wall of the nymphaeum.

25 – The Via Livenza Hypogeum

A short distance from the Via Salaria, on the Via Livenza, the humble gate of a garage leads to a small metal door which is the entrance to a subterranean monument known as the Via Livenza hypogeum. A dark and narrow stairway gives access to a room with a large basin separated from the rest of the area by a marble screen. Here the darkness turns to brightness, with iridescent glass mosaics and frescoes. On the back wall is a fresco whose whites, reds and blues merge in a chromatic dance featuring Artemis, the mistress of the woods and forests, represented as a queen with a diadem and laurel crown against a wooded backdrop at sunset as she is taking an arrow from her quiver, frightening a stag and doe. On the right-hand side of the wall, a young nymph in Artemis' retinue is leaning on her spear and petting a roe-deer. This lively fresco is divided into two sections by a niche–originally used to house a statue–painted with imitation Numidian marble squares. This geometric pattern is crowned by a scene with two doves drinking from a fountain (*kantharos*).

The sunken basin below this decorated wall is rectangular and deep, with steps used for immersion. On the first step (1.15 metres below ground level) are burial inscriptions for soldiers of the Praetorian Guard. Opposite these is the drainage hole and next to it is a sort of sluice gate for the flowing water.

Everything here seems to indicate this was a nymphaeum. But who would have used such an inhospitable and damp place, such a long and narrow room, for his baths or nymphaeum? Some small fresco scenes of putti playing and fishing on the register at left just above the basin may provide an answer. One putto is swimming, pulling a swan along with him by the neck while the poor creature tries to free itself, and another one seated on a rock is amusing himself by trying to spear a fish or octopus with his trident. Others are on boats with fishing nets, accompanied by aquatic birds. This marine scene is a complement to the upper register, which is a mosaic with multicoloured glass tesserae. In this lat-

Opposite: detail of the frescoed register, with putti playing and fishing.

ter we can barely make out the lower section, with two figures, one standing and the other kneeling in front of a cliff from which water is gushing. At first sight it seems to be the famous biblical episode in which St. Peter, like Moses, makes water spurt from a rock, but in this case in order to baptize a converted centurion. If this were so, the scene would be one of the most ancient scenes of baptism by immersion. But how can we justify the presence of Diana the huntress? What role would she play in a sanctuary of initiation into Christianity?

To solve this matter, some scholars have claimed that the figure of Diana as a huntress is a symbol of paganism who drives away the deer (potential Chistians) from the font and kills them. According to this theory, the nymph caressing the roe-deer is a person receptive to Christianity, so much so that she is a sort of *nympha sancti Petri* connected to a famous site outside Rome: *ad nymphas Santi Petri ubi baptizavit.*

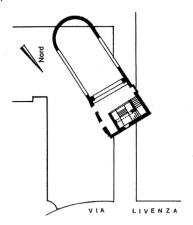

Above: plan of the monumental complex.
Opposite: the hall with the pool and frescoed back wall.

But what kind of building is this? What mystery lies hidden behind these curious representations? Another bold theory claims that it is the sanctuary of a mystery cult whose primary ritual consisted in diving or immersion in water. The devotees of this cult, known for their debauchery, were called *Baptai*, from the word *bapto* or "I immerse myself". And in fact their diving in water was a form of liberation, somewhat like an estatic, rapturous alteration of consciousness. The word *Baptai* means "immersed in water", that is to say, practitioners of *baptisma*, and the group, with its orgiastic practices, had as its chief deity the Thracian goddess Bendis, whom some call a "crude demon" and others a "guide of the shameless". One point in favour of this theory is that the goddess Bendis (often associated with another Thracian goddess, Kotys) was, as Herodotus himself tells us, assimilated with the Greek Artemis.

26 – The Hypogeum of the Flavians

One of the largest catacombs in Rome contains an ancient Roman burial complex that is traditionally ascribed to the imperial Flavians, who were Christians. This grandiose and luxurious complex is one of the most ancient and interesting in the Domitilla cemetery. It was discovered in 1865 by Michele Stefano de Rossi, who described it enthusiastically: "Convinced that the Christian cemetery was there, I wanted to go underground from the Sacripanti vineyard, which occupies this rise. I leave it to the reader to imagine my joy when, having ordered the diggers to look for an accessway to the underground chambers, they found a hole and, a short time later, an opening that led to a magnificent stairway, all plastered and decorated with frescoes."

Now entrance to the site is through a gallery that is connected to the labyrinth of branching passageways. There is nothing that would make us think this was a pagan burial site, since the recesses and intersecting galleries are to be found in other parts of the catacomb. But once inside the central gallery, we discover a series of frescoed panels on the walls, a myriad of aedicules and sections with red and green lines; and the many cupids, putti, dolphins and birds on the ceiling create a peaceful bucolic and marine atmosphere.

Apparently nothing is connected with Christianity here, except for a representation, on the lower section of the wall near the entrance, of Daniel in the guise of an orant, standing between two lions, and a dove flying toward Noah's Ark. However, this painting is on a layer of plaster added in a later period. If on the one hand we may describe the decorative motifs as rather vague, and thus suitable for both pagan and Christian use, this does not hold true for the paintings on the vault of the second niche from the entrance. This is neither naturalistic painting nor the idyllic-sacred type aiming at representing otherworldly beautitude, but is rather a clear-cut sequence of landscape scenes revolving around Priapus. The god of fertility

Opposite: one of the cubicula in the main gallery.

and virility stands out with his huge phallus among the Christian martyrs and their loculi and tombs. If this were not relegated to a minor position and in only one niche, the figure of Priapus would be offensive. But in fact the other niches have more conventional rural and pastoral motifs. It is therefore most probable that the hypogeum was originally pagan and was later adapted to the Christian religion. After leaving what was the original entrance, we come to the small square in front of it. The projecting section used as a vestibule is divided into several service rooms. When around the end of the 3rd or the beginning of the 4th century A.D. the hypogeum had become an integral part of the catacomb cemetery, a hall for funeral banquets was laid out to the right of the entrance; the masonry benches along the walls are the only remains of this. Here, during the *Parentalia* or *Feralia* celebrations for the dead, the elaborate *refrigeria* feasts were also held. To the left of the entrance, in fact, are the well and pipes that supplied water for this celebration.

To the right, after the meeting hall, one enters a small room with remains of a fresco of Eros and Psyche. The latter, voluptuous and attractive with her butterfly wings, is depicted gathering flowers with Eros in the peaceful Elysian Fields. This is a delicate fresco that in no way encroaches upon the tranquillity of the niche and the presence of the children who were buried there in ancient times.

Above: detail of the cubiculum fresco of Eros and Psyche.
Opposite: plan of the grandiose Flavian hypogeum complex.

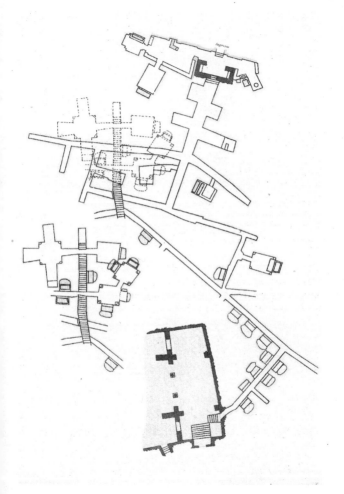

Insulae and Domus

Houses in ancient Rome developed vertically rather than horizontally because of problems of overpopulation. Consequently, if we consider the vast space taken up by the forums, temples, public gardens, etc., imperial Rome had a building density much more like the great cities of the East than the geometric configuration of the rationally planned *castra*. The *Regional Catalogues* tell us that during the Imperial Age the city had 46,602 *insulae* as opposed to 1,797 *domus*, a ratio of one to 26–a clear indication of the intense urban development of ancient Rome.

This was a city that had expanded chaotically and irrationally around dark, narrow alleyways and had developed upwards, with buildings that resembled our present-day tenements. "The majesty of Rome, the considerable growth of its population, led to the need to increase its dwellings in an extraordinary manner, and this very situation triggered the search for a solution by building upwards," says Vitruvius. Here one lived quite differently from those fortunate enough to have large, comfortable *domus* with their uniform layout: *fauces, atrium, alae, triclinium, tablinum* and *peristylium*.

These two kinds of habitation coexisted in Rome, the former greatly outnumbering the latter, as we have seen. Naturally, the aristocratic horizontal development of the one and the humble verticality of the other were clear signs of the economic and social status of their

Opposite: the area under S. Paolo alla Regola.

inhabitants. But whether one lived in a *domus* or an *insula*, life in Rome was an expensive matter. Even for modest rented flats the average price was considerably higher than that in the provinces. As Juvenal wrote, "The hard-up citizens of Rome should have emigrated in swarms long ago. Here it is very difficult for those with virtues to overcome the unsurmountable obstacle of a lack of money: in Rome all their efforts are in vain! A miserable apartment costs a pretty penny indeed, as does having servants or partaking of a humble supper."

Above: detail of the mosaic pavement, S. Paolo alla Regola subterranean area.
Opposite: the subterranean chamber known as the Room of the Column.

27 – The Aracoeli Insula

Tucked away in a corner at the foot of the Capitoline Hill is an *insula* made of ancient brickwork whose austerity is barely relieved by a small Romanesque campanile. It speaks to us of everyday life in ancient times, allowing us to visualize a different Rome, a city consisting not of monumental squares, forums, nymphaea, statues and columns, but narrow alleys and overcrowded apartment blocks.

Since it is hidden by the overwhelming monumentality of the Aracoeli and Campidoglio staircases, this *insula* is not an attraction for passers-by, who rarely note its presence. And yet it is one of the few surviving examples in Rome of a "normal" block of apartments, a true, well-preserved *insula* that has, besides its *tabernae* floor with a mezzanine, three storeys and traces of a fourth one.

The *insula* was built in the 4th century B.C. to meet the needs of a continuously growing population. Its layout was much like that of our modern buildings, and it was divided into several so-called *cenacula*, which were separate dwellings–similar to present-day ones–that were rented.

The *domus*, on the other hand, was a residence for the well-to-do that developed around a courtyard and had rooms such as the

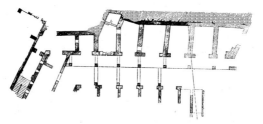

Above: plan of the first floor of the insula with a succession of rooms.
Opposite: hall on the second floor with brickwork.

atrium, the triclinium and the tablinum, each of which had a specific function.

The layout of an *insula* was as follows. The ground floor, when it did not consist of a single *domus*, was divided into a number of *tabernae* (storehouses or workshops) that were the workplace as well as the home of the tenant. He lived with his family in these narrow, poorly lit rooms. A small elevated area like a mezzanine was used as the bedroom; its only source of light was a window at the front of the *taberna*. The upper floors were taken up by several separate dwellings which became smaller the higher the storey, so that the top rooms were virtually uninhabitable. The façades of these tenements–which, as we have seen, were very much like our present-day ones–had balconies decorated with flowers, porticoes and loggias and were quite attractive. However, the interiors were extremely uncomfortable and the hygienic conditions were poor, to say the least.

By going back in time we can easily visualize this forgotten ruin when it was animated by crowds of noisy people, with tenants at their windows shouting to others in the alley, a tumultuous, infernal horde with "carts going up and down," as Juvenal tells us, "and the flocks stopping and making a racket that would awaken Drusus himself or a sea lion." No one seemed to have any regard for the poor inhabitants packed in the dark and ramshackle rooms on the upper floors. Juvenal provides a chilling description: "The third storey is already on fire and you know nothing about it. From the ground floor upward there is tumult, but the last one who will be roasted alive is the poor devil who is protected from the rain only by the roof tiles, where the doves come to lay their eggs."

Opposite: the hall on the first floor with some opus reticulatum *masonry.*

28 – The Ancient Roman House
   under the Barracco Museum

In the street named after the trunk makers and vendors, Via dei Baullari, there is a small building whose austere lines and harmonious proportions are in keeping with the best of Florentine Renaissance architecture. It was built in 1513 in the prevailing style as the residence of Tommaso Le Roy, a prelate in the papal court.

The Palazzetto ai Baullari, designed by an unknown architect, is a handsome edifice with 16th-century decoration that lies over the ruins of the Campus Martius. Behind the compact elegance of its rusticated masonry and graceful serlianas it houses a small but precious collection of antiquities consisting of unique and rare pieces that reflect the sophisticated taste of the person who spent so much of his life collecting them, Baron Giovanni Barracco.

The museum boasts Egyptian, Assyrian, Etruscan, Greek and Roman objects, thus giving visitors the opportunity to compare different styles and influences among the ancient Mediterranean civi-

Above: detail of fresco depicting a duck feeding.

Opposite: the portico, which has six columns with smooth shafts.

lizations. And in this prestigious context, the basement area is also a major attraction, since it contains the remains of a late Imperial Age building.

A wide stairway goes down about five metres to the remains of a building, whose function is unknown to us, that opens onto a portico that has six columns with smooth shafts. A facing of *opus vittatum* masonry, with its courses of bricks, goes around that series of columns and delimits the courtyard; a marble *labrum* with a hole in its base (which shows it was a fountain) lies against it. The rich and variegated marble pavement on different levels (denoting various building phases) heightens the elaborate decorative effect. Both the green-veined cipolin and *opus sectile* masonry with multicoloured, geometric patterns show that this pavement was intended for wealthy persons and that the building certainly had an important function (either private or public).

The fascinating marble decoration on the walls and the surviving

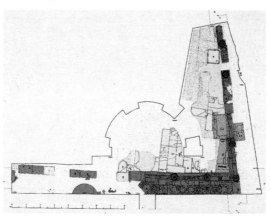

Above: plan of the Roman house indicating the various building phases.
Opposite: the portico; the marble labrum *was used as a fountain.*

frescoes leave no room for doubt concerning the luxuriousness of the furnishings. There are small rectangles with various scenes: graceful cupids fishing, a deer and lion hunt, a multicoloured duck with a snake in its beak in a lake landscape. The frescoes are not overly concerned with content, but aim at generic naturalistic rendering.

This edifice could easily be considered a rich patrician *domus* built in late antiquity, one of the many that stood in the western section of the Campus Martius, were it not for the presence of a marble slab for weighing and measuring that may indicate it had some public function. An erroneous interpretation of one of the fresco scenes led to the belief that this was a *statio* of one of the teams that competed in the circus, the "Prasina" or green team, which was really in Vicolo del Pavone. It is much more likely that the building was an emporium serving one of the most heavily populated central districts in Rome.

29 – Subterranean Structures at S. Paolo alla Regola

In the 16th-century walls around a group of small houses in the Regola district, there are fragments of ancient Roman masonry. At the end of the entrance hall is a small door leading to a stairway to the lower floor with two barrel-vaulted rooms of the same size–which originally looked onto an alley running parallel to the river–that date from the Flavian period. They are in fact remains of the huge food warehouse laid out during Domitian's rule, consisting of a series of storerooms arranged one over the other on two floors that was known as the *Horrea Vespasiani*. Going back up the stairs, we find ourselves in an area almost entirely occupied by a massive brick column. The walls bear traces of houses everywhere. One can make out the windows, the niches for the lanterns, and stairs, so it is logical to take this as a courtyard like so many others in ancient Rome.

But there are no statues, columns or coloured marble here, only modest dwellings for "commoners", a different dimension expressing the simple, rudimentary everyday life of a community of labourers and tradesmen. Adjacent to this, on the upper floor of the Domitian storerooms, are modest rooms with black and white mosaics with simple geometric patterns, and we can even make out the terracotta water pipes, which convey images of the ordinary life of these ancient people.

Behind two of the Severian period storerooms is another vast courtyard containing large fragments of plaster with imitation polychrome marble dressing painted on them. Archaeologists have found traces of what must have been a laundry (*fullonica*) and some interesting medieval finds–piles of amphorae, *Spondylus* shells and pigs' teeth. The presence in this area, during the Middle Ages and Renaissance, of several guilds–such as those of the tanners (who processed pigskin) and the metalsmiths or *caccabarii* (who made pots, kettles and pans)–bespeaks a custom dating back to ancient times and an economic-social continuity in this part of Rome in direct contact with the Tiber river.

Opposite: view of the rooms in the subterranean complex.

30 – The Domus Aurea

The emperor Nero wanted a house worthy of a sovereign, or better, "of a man", but his interpretation of these terms was based on a rather personal scale of values. His desire gave rise to a grandiose and impressive residence that branched out into the heart of the city, almost wholly occupying it. There was no lack of sarcastic comments about this, but Nero seems not to have worried about it, taken up as he was with emulating the pomp and glory of the Hellenistic rulers in the Middle East. "Rome will become his house: emigrate to Veio or Quiriti; that is, unless this house spreads all over Veio as well!"

Vainglory and a theocratic conception of the Roman Empire had indeed led the emperor to requisition a vast portion of the city and to map out an incredible plan to make a city in the form of a villa: the *Domus Aurea*, or Golden Residence. The designers and makers of this bold project were the architects Severus and Celer, who created a fantastically huge residence oriented to the cardinal points and laid out around huge parks and artificial lakes between the Esquiline, Palatine and Celian Hills, some sections even extending as far as the Velia. And they supplied the villa with dazzling technical innovations and precious furnishings and decoration. As Suetonius relates, "A colossal statue 120 feet high, the image of Nero, could fit in the vestibule of the house, the size of which was such as to include three mile-long porticoes, and a lake–or better, almost a sea–surrounded by edifices as large as a city. Behind this were villas with fields, vineyards and pasture, woods filled with all kinds of domestic and wild animals. In the other areas everything was covered in gold, ornated with gems and shells. The ceilings of the banquet halls were covered with movable sheets of ivory that were perforated to allow for cascades of flowers and perfumes. The most imporant hall was round and rotated continuously, day and night, just like the Earth. Both salt water and sulphurous water were channelled into the baths. When construction was completed and Nero inaugurated the edifice, he stated he was

Opposite: detail of the painted decoration in one of the halls.

satisfied and that he could finally live in a house worthy of a man."
The vestibule was located near the Temple of Venus and Roma, in front of the Colosseum, which at the time had not yet been built, while in the valley it now occupies there was an artificial lake. Other buildings with porticoes, gardens and countryside constituted a spectacular setting for the complex. Today only the dark, intricate halls in the pavilion on the Oppian Hill bear witness to its original grandiosity and vastness. A labyrinth of rooms, which are laid out in a more orderly fashion on the west side, surrounds a large rectangular courtyard, while the arrangement of those on the east side is more complicated, as they lie around a polygonal alcove, with the addition of an area that fans out from an octagonal hall. A seemingly interminable sequence of rooms and areas, in which cryptoporticuses, nymphaea and cubicula can be distinguished, almost makes us lose our bearing. Here there are amazing examples of that fantastic decoration that in the late Renaissance went under the name of "grotesque". And one can detect signs of Fabullus' soft, "floral" style, the richness of his decorative patterns, his fantastic, theatrical creations, so typical of the Fourth Style. From the gilded vault to the octagonal hall, one is spellbound by the play of colours, the fabulous inventiveness of this painter, and we can visualize the original colours, the gilded walls, the myriad examples of precious decoration. All this inevitably brings to mind the philosophical principles that inspired this sovereign who wanted to become a Sun god, with his cultural background permeated with Mazdaism and Mithraism and his worship of the Sun. Consequently, everything seems to follow a logical pattern, albeit an egocentric and eccentric one–from the calculated orientation of the rooms to the theatrical touches and the gilding. The very presence of the colossus in the entrance vestibule, Helios with the emperor's features, seems to be in keeping with this ideology and with the idea of an imperial residence as an *instrumentum regni*, a policy modelled after Middle Eastern customs whereby the prince becomes a sacred image, a divinity.

Opposite: the Laocoön group, *found in the Domus Aurea zone in 1506.*

Utility and Pleasure

In the preceding chapters it was possible to group the buildings and sites according to their common function, but in the descriptions that follow this will be difficult. The overall criterion of this chapter is to bring together constructions with different functions but which nonetheless can be categorized generically as public buildings, or better, buildings of public utility. Therefore, we have a wide range of complexes and structures that are quite different and yet fit under the general heading of "public architecture".

The latrines and cisterns show the high level of hydraulic engineering achieved in ancient Rome as well as the rational use of water under the management of carefully selected and highly specialized officials, the *curatores aquarum*. The sundial was a symbolic, propagandistic element but at the same time a useful tool for measuring time. Stadiums, as venues for public entertainment, were both vehicles of celebration and a means of attaining public consensus in keeping with the policy of *panem et circenses*. Prisons were no less useful and acceptable: the Mamertine prison, because of its strategic position, was the most representative and dreadful.

Thus we have a wide range of public architecture that meets the twofold need for utility and pleasure and offers a picture of Rome during the Imperial Age, with all its splendour and wretchedness.

Opposite: a passageway in the Stadium of Domitian.

31 – The Seven Halls

Among the hidden treasures in the Oppian Hill is one of the most important and gigantic cisterns in antiquity, known as the Seven Halls. This majestic and austere structure is a fine example of the ancient Romans' architectural and engineering genius, conforming to Vitruvius' principle of "solidity, utility and beauty." With the typical Roman pride in building necessary, solid and long-lasting works, Pliny the Elder compared this with "the useless and mad ostentation of the Pyramids." The rationale of this reservoir certainly did not escape notice. Stendhal, for example, included it in one of his walking tours of Rome. In December 1828 he visited those long, dark galleries covered with creeping plants, losing his way in the labyrinth of halls and corridors, among the damp walls coated with slime, and discovered that nothing here had been left to chance. Everything, down to the most minute detail, revealed the masterly skill of ancient Roman architecture: the calculated alignment of the halls, the *opus signinum*

facing, the absence of dead ends.

This was a well-planned complex designed to make the best use of a reservoir with a capacity of 8,165,000 litres of water fed by a branch of one of the aqueducts that took water to Rome via the Porta Maggiore and the Esquiline Hill, probably the Aqua Julia. It was a perfect mechanism for supplying water for the first large Roman baths, the Baths of Trajan, which were built by the architect Apollodorus of Damascus. The nymphaea, fountains and pools in these baths were fed by the impressive flow of water that only the destructive fury of the Ostrogoths managed to eliminate.

This cistern is embedded in the earth, so that only the brick façade of its two storeys are visible. Nine niches–corresponding to the same number of halls (when the structure was discovered, archaeologists found only seven halls, hence the name)– lend movement to the façade. Inside the niches on the lower floor one can see, at the top, the

The front of the grandiose "Seven Halls" cistern.

holes of the *fistulae* (water pipes), one on either side of the opening of the rectangular niches, and a central one in the semicircular niches. At the opening of each *fistula* was a lead plate nailed to the wall and also covered with *opus signinum* facing to prevent water seepage.

A steep iron stairway leads to the interior. Nine long, parallel halls form an enclosure with three straight sides and one curved wall. This latter, at the end of the large space, was curved so that the water supply would flow toward the drainage channel and avoid dead ends. Each gallery communicates with the other by means of four arches that were staggered in order to offer greater resistance to the pressure of the water flowing from one to the other, and also to avoid the creation of currents. The inflow conduit was in the middle of the curved back wall. From there the water flowed through the series of long galleries, which were made waterproof by the *opus signinum* facing.

The cistern was used at least up to the 5th century A.D. Some structures above the terrace were probably used as service rooms. In late antiquity a *domus* was built over the them; its remains can be seen above the cistern.

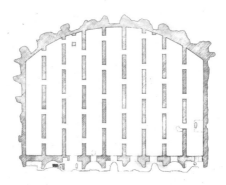

Above: plan of the cistern.
Opposite: the openings that link the various halls.

32 – The Ancient Roman Cistern
in Via Cristoforo Colombo

This large cylindrical brick structure is yet another link between past and present that is so characteristic of the urban fabric of Rome. Although it is surrounded by large buildings, and even high-risers, this monument to civil engineering still epitomizes the ancient Romans' ingenuity and will in building solid constructions that were at once useful and noble, able to resist the ravages of time. With their rational structure, cisterns, fountains and aqueducts were in fact the pride of the Romans, their rejoinder to Greek architecture, which was essentially based on aesthetic principles.

Exactly like other ancient Roman reservoirs, the one in Via Colombo must have lain partly or wholly below the ground. The fact that it now stands well above ground level is due the barbarous excavation works effected to lay out the Via Imperiale, now called Via Colombo—a scandalous operation that devastated the area and its ancient buildings and also brought about the underground diversion of the Almone river and the demolition of all the buildings along its banks. The considerable lowering of the ancient ground level uncovered the cistern, which lay beneath a farmhouse that had been built over the long-abandoned reservoir and was being demolished.

Thus two huge cylindrical structures were gradually brought to light, the largest of which was identified as a cistern; it had a large round outer shell and concentric corridors made of *opus reticulatum* masonry dating from the 2nd century A.D. The first ring has ten spaces that are connected to one another by arches, while in the inner ambulatory the vault is divided into bays by five arches. All this creates a regular architectural rhythm that is quite fascinating. Iron stairs lead to the interior, into a sort of vestibule that is barrel-vaulted and irregular in shape, with some sections covered with *opus signinum* masonry. This is followed by what seems to be an endless sequence of curved bays that envelops and captivates one with its

Opposite: the innermost ambulatory; the vault is divided into bays by five arches.

skillful, creative architecture. The bays and inner ring corridor are linked by arches and openings that merge the halls in an intricate maze of spaces that dazzle one with their curvilinear rhythm.

This fascinating winding course almost makes us forget all the technical details concerning the waterproofing, the construction of the vaults and the masteful use of bricks a foot and a half long. But this is a fine piece of hydraulic engineering, as is evident in the solid and efficient construction, the waterproof *opus signinum* dressing, and the use of curbs to round off sharp corners. Contrary to what one might expect, the cistern did not supply water to a villa (no ruins of

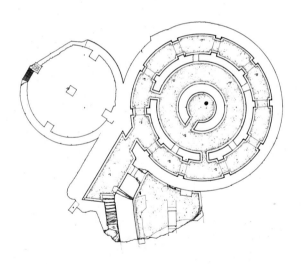

Above: plan of the cistern, with its succession of concentric corridors.

Opposite: the outer shell of the cistern (2nd century A.D.), in opus reticulatum.

which were found), but its water was channelled to the fields of a large landed estate by means of an aqueduct. It lies in the suburbs of Rome and the area is distinguished by its many tombs, funerary monuments, villas and estates. The chance discovery of this huge cistern bears witness to the architectural skill and resources of the ancient Romans, who created an eloquent and noble ruin that quite overshadows the modern high-risers nearby.

33 – Augustus' Sundial

The proud Obelisk of Psammetichus II (early 6th century B.C.) towers over the Chamber of Deputies and casts its shadow over Piazza di Montecitorio. It came from Heliopolis, Egypt and Augustus had it transported to the Campus Martius to make it the pointer (gnomon) of his majestic sundial. This slender 21.80-metre obelisk commemorated the emperor's conquest of Egypt. It indicated the hours, days, season cycles, winds and astral influences on a large travertine plate or base. As a symbol of the cosmos it marked time in homage to the emperor. As Pliny writes, "The divine Augustus attributed miraculous powers to the obelisk in the Campus Martius; that is to say, he believed it was able to capture the sun's shadow and determine the length of the days and nights. Consequently, he ordered a pavement

Above: the obelisk of Psammetichus II seen from below.
Opposite: detail of the marble relief of Augustus' Ara Pacis.

made of slabs whose width was proportionate to the height of the obelisk, so that the shadow would be equal to this pavement on the sixth hour [noon] of the winter solstice and, little by little, day by day, would decrease and then increase once again, indicated by bronze markers set into the pavement. It is worth noting that this was the work of the astronomer Novius Facundus, who added a gilded globe to the top of the obelisk so that the shadow would gather on its summit and thus prevent the apex from casting too long a shadow, drawing his inspiration, so it is said, from the human head."

To make the sundial (10 B.C.), the emperor summoned astronomers and mathematicians from Alexandria, who with erudition and ability harnessed time into a schematic grid marked out on the square by bronze markers, thus conceiving a quadrant whose metal strips produced geometric, astral and sacred configurations. This was not only an instrument for measuring, but a monument to the sun, the stars and Augustus' *aurea aetas*, or golden age. On September 23, Augustus' birthday and the day of the autumn equinox, the pointed shadow of the gnomon, with a clearly commemorative and theatrical

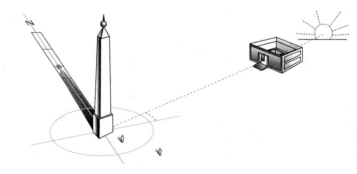

Above: drawing showing the alignment of Augustus' sundial with the Ara Pacis.
Opposite: the Ara Pacis.

effect, extended to the middle of the Ara Pacis (Altar of Peace), thus symbolically marking the divine birth of the emperor, whom destiny had chosen to inaugurate a new era of peace and grandeur for Rome and its empire. Furthermore, the pink granite obelisk was laid out in such a way that one of its sides should face the rising sun on April 21, the day when Rome was founded. Everything was therefore carefully planned to highlight and enhance the divine destiny of the birth of the first person who would be honoured with the title of "Augustus," a sacred destiny fixed by the stars and sanctioned by the sun.

Nothing remains of that celebrative square, which was about 160 metres wide from east to west and 75 metres long from north to south. There is only a tiny fragment left of that desire to mark the hours by equating the majesty of the cosmos with that of the emperor: a piece of marble that still has the bronze rules, discovered eight metres under the ground in a cellar in no. 48 Via del Campo Marzio. This room is reached from a small courtyard by means of a ladder, but is well worth your while. Set between the signs of Virgo and Aries is a Greek inscription: *Etesiai Pauontai* ("The Etesian winds are abating").

34 – The Stadium of Domitian

In distant 86 A.D., Piazza Navona–then without the characteristic sound of Bernini's fountains–was chosen by the emperor Domitian as the site of a stadium where imperial Rome could imitate the Greeks with its own *Agon Capitolinus*, a wide range of competitions held every four years that included artistic and literary events as well as sports. The games called for an alternation of sports and the arts, so that a foot race was coupled with a rhetoric competition, followed by boxing and Latin poetry, the discus throw and Greek poetry, and the javelin throw and music.

The Agon conceived by Domitian was included in the programme of Rome's festivals with an elaborate ceremony that commenced with a lavish inauguration in the presence of the emperor who, for the occasion, "wore sandals and a purple Greek toga, his head bearing a golden crown with the images of Jupiter, Juno and Minerva, while around him were seated the Flamen Dialis priest and the priest of the Flavians, all dressed in the same manner, except for the fact that their crowns bore the emperor's portrait." (Suetonius).

Besides the stadium (*circus agonalis*), another venue was needed for the many games: the odeum, used for the music competitions, recitations and poetry competitions. Both these edifices have been preserved in the modern city, which proudly maintains their original plan. Piazza Navona lies over the field of the ancient stadium and nearby Palazzo Massimo alle Colonne, designed in a singular manner by Peruzzi, is modelled after the original theatre shape of the ancient odeon. Judging by the seating capacity of the two structures–15,000 for the odeon and 30,000 for the stadium–these games must have been extremely popular with the citizens of Rome. However, these figures are nothing compared with the crowds that thronged the amphitheatres (the Colosseum alone could seat 80,000 spectators). It must be said that this difference in popularity was due not only to the different type of spectacle

Opposite: the walls supporting the tiers of the stadium.

involved–gladiatorial combat as opposed to rhetoric contests, for example. It also involved a certain measure of puritanical chauvinism that looked down on the "imported" athletic games and the fact that the athletes were nude. The ancient Romans disapproved of the Greek contests held in the *Agon Capitolinus*, even the intellectuals, who considered the gladiatorial combats in the amphitheatres bloody and cruel. Cicero endorsed the Latin poet Ennius' statement that "scandal begins when one bares his body before his fellow citizens," and for his part Tacitus said: "This was all we needed: they make a public show of their nakedness, put on the boxers' cestus and think about those combats instead of military service." But the final blow was delivered by Seneca, with his disdainful view of the athletes: "What feeble souls have those whose muscles and shoulders we so admire."

The stadium was about 275 metres long and 106.10 metres wide and had two straight sides and one curved one. The exterior was austere and majestic with its rows of columns and arcades, where various commercial activities flourished, from the sale of merchandise to prostitution.

The exterior consisted of two superposed rows of arches supported by travertine pillars that alternated with statues and other decoration, thus lending dignity and monumentality to the construction. From a balcony in Piazza Tor Sanguigna one can see the stadium and visualize its original size, because there are still the remains of one of the main entrances with its travertine arcade and the ruins of the porch opposite, which has a mutilated column made of *porta-santa* marble.

One can descend 3.5 metres below ground level into the subterranean area, where an entire section of the ancient cavea of the stadium is in a perfect state of preservation. We can observe the structure with its rhythm of alternating passageways and halls, appreciate it as an architectural achievement, and visualize the vivacious, colourful games taking place in the arena, with the enthusiastic crowd seated on the tiers.

35 – A Latrine in Via Garibaldi

Already in the early Imperial Age the ancient Romans showed their ability to construct beautiful, useful and ingenious works of architecture. As Strabo said, "The Romans concentrated mostly on what they [the Greeks] had neglected: paving streets, channelling water, building sewers that could drop all the city's waste into the Tiber [...] there is enough water conveyed by the aqueducts to make rivers flow through the city and the underground conduits."

However, the city sewers had never been connected to the apartments in the *insulae*. Except for the wealthy inhabitants of the *domus*, who had their own private latrines, all the other Romans had to use public latrines (*foricae*), which they had to pay for. In fact, the public latrines were managed by tax officials, the *conductores foricarum*. For the most part they were very pleasant places where people often came to meet and even get themselves invited to dinner: "Vacerra frequents all the latrines, / now one, then another, / where he sits and wiles away the day. / His great desire is to eat, not to defecate." (Martial).

People sat on benches, leaning against corbels sculpted in the shape of dolphins, surrounded by mosaic or painted decoration, in the midst of statues, stuccowork and small fountains. Naturally, the lower classes did not frequent these luxurious places but had to content themselves with jars, which were useful for the fullers, who always had a ready supply of urine for their trade.

One of these public latrines was discovered in 1963 after the collapse of a supporting wall of the square in front of S. Pietro in Montorio church. This edifice still has its fine painting decoration and bears witness to the organization of a public service system in ancient times. The waste drain can still be seen, and the lack of recesses in the walls probably indicates that the fittings were made of wood. Two sections of painted plaster on the walls make for a lovely decorative effect. It would almost seem like being in a living room, if it were not for the inscriptions and graffiti on the walls, which remind us that the place was in fact a urinal and public latrine, with its coarse and obscene atmosphere.

Detail of the layer of plaster with candelabra decorative motifs.

36 – The VII Militia Cohort

There were two Romes. One was the ostentatious, grandiose city
with its forums, temples, bronze equestrian statues, coloured marble,
squares surrounded by colonnades, statues and fountains; the other
was a city made of bricks and wood, crushed into small spaces and
narrow alleyways, packed in large tenements. The second Rome
belonged to the working class and was the result of chaotic urban
growth, the *insulae* made of poor building material and crowded
together in small spaces so that they could only go upward five or
six storeys. Sometimes this height was achieved without bothering
about the solidity of the structure, and collapses were quite common.
"At Prenaeste, which is so cool," writes Juvenal, "at Bolsena, amid
the wooded hills, or in peaceful Gabi or on the sloping hill of Tivoli,
who would ever fear that his house would fall on him? But we want
to live in a city held up for the most part by insecure beams because
the administrator knows no other way of sustaining walls; and when
he has filled in the old cracks, he tells us to have sweet dreams–with
that constant danger overhead."

The use of wood for the ceilings, the room partitions and the fittings was a constant threat to the very survival of houses and tenants alike. The corridors that were supposed to serve as fire barriers
were virtually useless, since portable stoves, candles, oil-lamps and
torches were used continuously in these dwellings. "While trying to
save what little he has, Ucalegon shouts for them to bring water; and
beneath him the third floor is in flames." (Juvenal). Water was very
scarce in the tenements and in general only the privileged few on the
ground floor could afford to pay the high sum asked for it. Certainly,
it would have been wiser to follow Juvenal's advice: "It is much better to live where there are never any fires and one can sleep at night
without terror always striking one's heart."

In the meantime, the emperor Augustus had established a true military corps in 6 A.D.: the new *vigiles* militia, whose duty was to fight
fires and patrol the neighbourhoods against burglars, thieves and
fences. This corps, headed by a *praefectus vigilum*, was organized

into seven cohorts which in turn were divided into seven centuries. Since Rome in Augustus' time was divided into fourteen districts, each cohort patrolled two districts, setting up their garrison headquarters (*statio*) in one and a barracks with a detachment of guards (*excubitorium*) in the other.

The only surviving building is the smaller barracks of the permanent detachment of the VII cohort, the one responsible for the XIV District (present-day Trastevere). This was an underground building constructed in the late 2nd century A.D. over a private residence. A stairway leads to the interior, a hall barely illuminated by some windows high up along the walls. These latter, faced in brick, bear signs of the ancient mouldings and the architect's ambition in a building with a clear-cut functional use. A large mosaic pavement with white and black tesserae once covered the entire hall with an aquatic dance of Tritons and sea monsters celebrating their triumph over fire. This whirling dance was interrupted by a hexagonal pool that attracted attention to the opposite wall and its portal, which heralded a probable *genius exubitorii* (shrine to the protective genii

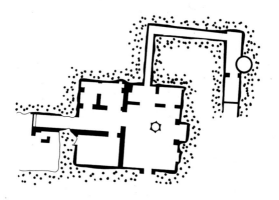

Plan of the barracks. The atrium with the pool is in the middle.

of the barracks). Next to the main hall is a series of service rooms, one of which seems to have been a bath. Densely packed graffiti on the plaster bore the names of the militia guards, their fears, supersitions and descriptions of their hard work, carried out with a few, rudimentary implements: poles, ladders, ropes and special blankets (*centomes*) that were soaked in water and used to quench fires. The guards had special pumps (*siphones*) to draw water through the pipes. Lacking this, they had to rely on their sheer physical strength, passing water buckets lined with pitch (*vasa spartea*) or containers known as *hamae* from one to the other. The graffiti also relate the fatigue and dangers of night duty, and the difficulties of the *serbaciarii*, who had the task of preparing the torches for the night patrols to ensure some degree of safety to the inhabitants. "You may die as many times as there are windows open facing the street as you pass at night," says Juvenal. "You can only hope, and hold fast to this miserable hope, that those windows will do no more than throw the contents of their basins onto your head."

The hexagonal pool in the atrium.

Glossary

Acrolith A wooden statue covered with drapery except for the extremities. The head, arms and legs could be of marble, stone or ivory.

Agape Mithraic ritual banquet.

Ambulatory 1. A covered passageway. 2. In medieval churches, an aisle, usually semicircular, that runs between the apse and the altar.

Apse The vaulted end, either semicircular or polygonal, of a chancel or chapel of a Christian church. It was also an element of Roman architecture.

Atrium 1. In Etruscan or Roman houses, a sort of peristyle courtyard that led to the rooms proper. 2. In Christian basilicas, the porticoed entrance courtyard. 3. More generally, the monumental entrance to churches and palaces.

Basilica A Roman building with a rectangular plan used for public administration, with an apse at the end of the nave. The Christian basilica was based on this Roman structure.

Cella The innermost part of a temple, corresponding to the Greek *naos*, which contains the statue of the god worshipped therein.

Cipolin Marble with parallel stripes, from whitish-grey to dark green.

Cenaculum (cenacle) A dining room. Also the room(s) on the upper floor, the attic, or poor people's homes.

Circus An elongated Roman constuction for chariot races, one of the short ends being semicircular. It was characterized by the *spina* in the middle, a long wall with two columns or obelisks at its ends which was the turning post the chariots had to go around.

Crypt In ancient Greece and Rome, a hidden, subterranean place. In Christian churches, the chamber beneath the presbytery containing the graves or relics of martyrs.

Cryptoporticus An ambulatory or gallery in Roman architecture that was totally or partly concealed and had openings instead of columns.

Cubiculum 1. The bedroom in ancient Roman houses. 2. The burial chamber, or loculus, in catacombs.

Excubitorium Detachment of a cohort.

Fistula A water-pipe in ancient times.

Forum The main square in a Roman city, usually bounded by colonnades, where the major civic activities took place.

Gnomon The pointer indicating the hour on a sundial.

Groin (or cross) vault A vault produced by the intersection of two barrel vaults, thus forming four sides.

Hexastyle A temple or other building with six columns on the façade.

Hypogeum An underground vault or room with various functions.

Lararium A small shrine dedicated to the lares, or household deities.

Mausoleum A large monumental funerary structure, the name of which derives from the tomb of King Mausolus of Caria (350 B.C.) at Halicarnassus.

Nave The longitudinal interior of a church divided by walls, columns or piers.

Obelisk A tapering, four-sided monolithic stone pillar of Egyptian origin with a commemorative function.

Octastyle A temple or building with eight frontal columns.

Odeon A roofed building similar to a small theatre used for concerts and poetry readings in antiquity.

Opus mixtum (mixed work) A type of ancient Roman masonry using various techniques to reinforce *opus reticulatum* walling, with horizontal bands of bricks with lateral toothing added to frame the network pattern.

Opus reticulatum Ancient Roman walling that is faced with squared stones arranged diagonally in a network pattern.

Opus sectilis Paving consisting of slabs–mostly of marble but sometimes with other materials as well–that are cut into various, usually geometric shapes.

Opus signinum Ancient Roman masonry, a mixture of crushed brick (or terracotta), sand and lime.

Opus spicatum A type of ancient Roman masonry with stones and bricks arranged in a herringbone pattern.

Opus tessellatum Mosaic work consisting of variously arranged cubic tesserae made of stone, marble or vitreous paste.

Opus vittatum A type of ancient Roman masonry consisting of horizontal layers of bricks alternating with tufa blocks arranged in horizontal bands.

Peperino Greyish, mottled tufa of volcanic origin.

Peristyle A colonnade surrounding an inner court, behind which are the various rooms of an ancient Roman dwelling.

Sacellum In ancient Rome, a small unroofed space with an altar dedicated to a divinity. In Christian religious architecture, a small isolated church or a chapel in a large church.

Statio A Roman military guard house, or a barracks.

Tablinum A room in an ancient Roman house situated in the part of the atrium facing the entrance and used to store family records, documents and the like.

Travertine Marble quarried near Tivoli that was commonly used in Roman architecture.

Triclinium The dining room in an ancient Roman house with the typical triclinium couch.

Essential Bibliography

U. Bianchi (ed.), *Mysteria Mithrae*, Proceedings of the International Seminar "The Historic-religious Specificity of the Mithraic Mysteries, with Particular Reference to the Documentary Sources in Rome and Ostia," Leiden, 1979.

U. Bianchi, *La tipologia storica dei misteri di Mitra*, in: "Aufstieg und Niedergang der romischen Welt", II, 17, 4, Berlin-New York, 1984.

J. Carcopino, *La vita quotidiana a Roma all'apogeo dell'Impero*, Bari, 1982.

F. Castagnoli, *Topografia di Roma antica*, in: *Enciclopedia Classica*, III, 10, 3, Turin, 1954.

F. Coarelli, *Guida archeologica di Roma*, Rome, 1974.

L. Crema, *L'architettura romana*, in: *Enciclopedia Classica*, III, 12, 1, Turin, 1959.

F. Cumont, *Textes et monuments figurés relatifs aux mystères de Mithra*, I-II, Brussels, 1896-98.

F Cumont, *The Mysteries of Mithra*, Dover Publications Inc., 1956.

J. Darmesteter, *Le Zend-Avesta*, Paris, 1892. I. Della Porta, *Roma Sotterranea: le città sotto la città*, Newton-Compton, Rome, 1996. *Enciclopedia dell'Arte Antica*, Roma, vol. VI, Rome, 1965.

G. Lugli, *I monumenti antichi di Roma e suburbia*, vols. I-III and supplements, Rome, 1931-40.

G. Lugli, *Itinerario di Roma antica*, Milan, 1970.

G. Lugli, *Roma antica. Il centro monumentale*, Rome, 1946.

R. Merkelbach, *Mithras*, Konigstein, 1984. *Mithraic Studies. Proceedings of the First International Congress of Mithraic Studies, 1971*, I-II, Manchester, 1975.

A. Von Prònay, *Mitra*, Florence, 1991.

J;M.C. Toynbee, *Morte e sepoltura nel mondo romano*, Rome, 1933.

C. W. Weber, *Panem et circenses*, Milan, 1989.

HISTORIC SOURCES

Apuleius, *Metamorphóseon libri XI* (*Le Metamorfosi*, Rizzoli, Milan 1977).

Ausonius, *Epistulae, XXXI* (*Epistole*, Il Cardo, Venice 1995).

Cicero, *Tusculanae* (*Toscolane*, Paravia, Turin 1984).

Firmicus Maternus, *De errore profanarum religionum*, La Nuova Italia, Florence 1969.

J.W. Goethe, *Italienische Reise* (*Viaggio in Italia*, Rizzoli, Milan 1991).

Horace, *Carminum libri* (*Odi Epodi*, Garzanti, Milan 1986).

Horace, *Sermonum libri* (*Satire*, Garzanti, Milan 1976).

Justin, *I Apologia* (*Le due Apologie*, Edizioni Paoline, Rome 1983).

Juvenal, *Saturae* (*Satire*, Rizzoli, Milan 1989).

Titus Livy, *Ab Urbe Condita Libri* (*Storia di Roma*, Rizzoli, Milan 1982).

Macrobius, *Saturnaliorum libri* (*I Saturnali*, UTET, Turin 1967).

Martial, *Epigrammata* (*Epigrammi*, Garzanti, Milan 1984).

Ovid, *Fastorum libri* (*I Fasti*, Zanichelli, Bologna 1983).

Ovid, *Metamorphoséon libri* (*Le Metamorfosi*, Bompiani, Milan 1989).

A. Palladio, *I quattro libri dell'architettura*, Heopli, Milan 1980.

Plautus, *Mostellaria* (*Mostellaria - Persa*, Mondadori, Milan 1981).

Pliny, *Naturalis Historia* (*Storia Naturale*, Einaudi, Turin 1985).

Polybius, *Historiae* (*Storie*, Mondadori, Milan 1970).

Porphyry, *De anto nympharum* (*L'antro delle ninfe*, Adelphi, Milan 1986).

Sallust, *De coniuratione Catilinae* (*La congiura di Catilina*, Mursia, Milan 1993).

Seneca, *Epistulae morales* (*Epistole morali*, Dante Alighieri, Rome 1990).

Suetonius, *De vita duodecim caesarum libri VIII* (*Vita dei Cesari*, Rizzoli, Milan 1993).

Tacitus, *Annales* (*Gli Annali*, Garzanti, Milan 1983).

Tertullian, *De baptismo*, Paravia, Turin 1968.

Tertullian, *De Corona*, Mondadori, Milan 1992.

Vitruvius, *De Architectura* (*I dieci libri dell'architettura*, SugarCo, Varese 1990).

191